# STALWART LOT RAT

# Used-Car Finance Mastery

## Scott Carlson

Promulgate Press

Copyright © 2016 by Scott Carlson

Editing by Heidi Wallenborn

Cover design by Daria Lacy

Cover image (rat) by Sujono sujono/Shutterstock

Cover image (mouse trap) by dedMazay/Shutterstock

Special quantity discounts may be available for this title. For bulk purchase questions go to www.StalwartLotRat.com or call 817-605-8770 ext. 712

**Publisher Disclaimer**

The opinions, claims, and information contained in this book do not come from the publisher. The publisher makes no warranties or representations with respect to the accuracy or completeness of the contents of this book and disclaim any implied warranties of merchantability or fitness for a particular purpose. The information in this book may not be suitable for your situation and you should consult with an appropriate professional regarding your situation or any questions you may have. The publisher shall not be liable for any damage or loss whatsoever.

Published in the United States of America by Promulgate Press

ISBN: 978-0-692-72418-7

Interview, transcription, and editing assistance provided by BookByInterview.com

# Author Disclaimer

This book is designed to provide information on the used-car financing industry and the author's lifetime business and personal experiences only. This information is provided and sold with the knowledge that the publisher and author do not offer any legal or other professional advice. In the case of a need for any such expertise consult with the appropriate professional. This book does not contain all information available on the subject. This book has not been created to be specific to any individual's or organizations' situation or needs. Every effort has been made to make this book as accurate as possible. However, there may be typographical and or content errors. Therefore, this book should serve only as a general guide and not as the ultimate source of subject information. This book contains information that might be dated and is intended only to educate and entertain. The author and publisher shall have no liability or responsibility to any person or entity regarding any loss or damage incurred, or alleged to have incurred, directly or indirectly, by the information contained in this book. You hereby agree to be bound by this disclaimer.

# Table of Contents

# ACKNOWLEDGEMENTS

First and foremost, I would like to thank my Lord for everything.

I want to thank my beautiful wife of twenty-two years, Carroll Ann, for her love for me, commitment to our marriage, and enduring the challenges that come with being married to a serial entrepreneur.

Thank you to my entire family for loving me, and friends, mentors, clients, and fellow believers. You all have made varied and important contributions to my life.

Thank you to all who had any part, big or small, in helping the Carlson family succeed in buy-here pay-here over the decades.

Thank you to the team that I work with every day that makes it possible for me to exercise my entrepreneurship and also challenged me to write this book.

Thank you Kenny Atcheson of DealerProfitPros.com for reaching out to me at a national used-car dealer conference a number of years ago and becoming my dear friend. Writing this book with your team has helped me grow in ways that I never would have expected.

# PREFACE

S o what's with the rat, the cheese, and the trap on the cover?

I am glad you asked.

When I was a kid, one of my elementary school teachers had me color a rat that had escaped a trap, taking with him a big hunk of cheese. I still have that coloring page today.

At the time, the picture told me that this rat was able to get the big cheese; he was smart and he wasn't interested in crumbs.

When determining how to title this book, I found myself focused on how hard it was to start out in buy-here pay-here as a lot rat. Then I thought of all of the challenges and traps of the used-car finance business and what it takes to master the business.

That led me to my memory of the rat that I had colored. It had no interest in crumbs or leftovers – only the big piece of cheese. I started as a "lot rat" in my family's first dealership. Being stalwart allowed me to master the used-car finance business – hence the title of this book, *Stalwart Lot Rat / Used-Car Finance Mastery.*

My goal with this book is to make you aware of the challenges ahead and to help you master the used-car finance business.

Sincerely,

Scott Carlson

P.S. If you relate to any of following "stalwart" synonyms, this book is a must-read for you.

*dependable, fearless, indomitable, intrepid, redoubtable, staunch, tenacious, bold, bound, brave, daring, powerhouse, solid, steamroller, tough, athletic, bound and determined, brick-wall, courageous, dead set on, forceful, gutsy, hanging tough, muscular, nervy, robust, rugged*

# INTRODUCTION

One big passion that motivates me has roots in my heart that are as old as I am. I was raised in poverty. I hated living that way. I grew determined to do something about it in my life.

I have a heart for people who struggle in poverty. Beyond my childhood experience in poverty, it is tied to the buy-here pay-here space. I have a heart for people who are good folks who have good intentions, but maybe poor means.

My big passion is to help used-car financing dealerships to sell more cars and reduce repo losses because I know the struggles they go through to grow their businesses. In our family's dealership we mastered how to overcome challenges and embrace opportunity through the years. Helping other stalwarts to succeed gives me a sense of purpose.

Some of the most interesting things that occur in life are conversations. I have had many conversations with a good number of high-profile people who wanted to know my story. From start to finish I'd tell them how I came from poverty to ending up in some pretty phenomenal, high net-worth situations.

So many of those people told me, "You hafta tell your story. You have got to write a book." When I asked, "Why?"

they said that my story is inspiring and could help many people in many ways to understand what we all have to go through to succeed in life and in business, and to motivate a lot of people. So I decided to write a book.

After I began the process and have been thinking through things, I started to see how others will view my life from a written, documented point of view. When we look back on our lives and verbally tell our stories to people, it's different. In print, we start to see it. We get a picture of how somebody could benefit from what happened to us. I realized that I do have a lot to say and I believe what I know and have experienced in the used-car finance business through the last 45 years can help anyone in business, and specifically the guys in the buy-here pay-here industry.

In this book, you will find tips about the industry and what it takes to win. There is information about how to be an entrepreneur and what it takes to succeed and how you've got to push against all odds to get out of life what you want. There is a lot of that in this book.

But there are also stories about pulling myself up at a young age to be resourceful and successful. This book will also help young entrepreneurs just starting out to understand the sometimes rough and painful road ahead and how to come out stronger.

Until we've been through things, the younger we are, say under age 18, we think we're pretty bulletproof because our noses haven't been bloodied. When we get into business, especially in big business, we not only get our noses bloodied, but our heads bashed in and the wind pushed out of us when we get knocked down.

But we hafta get back up. Lying there was not an option for me. Failure happens when we lie there. We hafta take risks in order to win.

We learn by mistakes. If we're not making mistakes, we're not doing anything. Making mistakes is required in order to grow, to become bigger and maybe better than what we already were.

When I was going through the school of hard knocks and my family's buy-here pay-here business and later my indirect lending business was growing at a very fast pace, there was not really anybody to turn to for consulting. However, in the industry today there are industry trade show conferences, there are Twenty Groups, and there's a lot of information out there to lean on. My book is another way that somebody in the buy-here pay-here business can get information from an expert to help them over some hurdles rather than charge through all of the challenges like a bull.

You can go through the pain alone if you want to. You can do that and still succeed because there's enough profit margin in the industry to allow for the mistakes you're going to make. But why go through those? Learn from professionals. Learn from the guys who have already been there. Learn from someone like me who has developed tools to make your life easier.

High on the scale of things that bring you success as an entrepreneur is that you must be open. You must have an open mind toward anything that could possibly accelerate you in business or help you get off the ground. Don't be close-minded. You increase your chances of failing if you are close-minded.

More than anything else, persistence helped me be successful in business. Sometimes I just had to put blinders on. I ignored family member opinions that did not line up with my intuition, and I didn't let naysayers tell me, "That won't work, you can't do that."

Of course, you must be diligent and smart about what you're doing. Be realistic. Keep what you're doing and what you're going through realistic. Don't be a pie-in-the-sky dreamer and have ridiculous ideas about things that are most likely improbable. When you have your blinders on and you're on a good track, be persistent and consistent.

One last piece of advice before you discover the treasures buried throughout this book: to the degree that you're able, in whatever industry you are, do your best to move away from being a personality-driven business and into more of a systems-driven business. It's a lot easier to exponentially grow a systems-driven business than a personality-driven business.

Keep reading to find out why.

# CHAPTER ONE:

## Rough Beginnings and Early Exposure

My paternal grandmother Henrietta was a 350-pound German lady who came from Germany to New York on a ship in the late 1800s. She met my Swedish grandfather, Karl Carlson, who had also come over on a ship. They both wanted a new life in America.

Grandfather Carlson was a carpenter — a master framer of houses — that's what a lot of Swedish immigrants did in those days. Grandmother had done some opera singing. They were an odd pairing, but somehow they got together to start a family and landed in Narrowsburg, New York, which had a population of less than 500 people.

Being an immigrant, my grandfather followed his country's tradition and taught my father and his two brothers the same trade as his father had taught him. They were expected to follow in the family trade.

But my father, Kent "Mike" Carlson, grew up hating construction and hated working outdoors. He wanted out but couldn't find a way. So he resigned himself to carpentry.

They all had a very dysfunctional relationship as a family. My grandmother dominated the entire family and ruled it with an iron fist via verbal abuse and fear tactics. Because of the dysfunction that defined my father's family, he grew up to be a narcissistic, miserable person in spite of his good fortune. He had horrible personal morals. This in turn led to a lot of dysfunction in the family that I grew up in which I am glad to say time, death and maturity has resolved.

All of that being said, I must say my father had great business ethics which he passed on to his sons. He taught us that we should treat all people the same regardless of their social economic circumstances, we should always do what we say we are going to do when we say we are going to do it, under-promise and over-deliver, and that being on time is all about respect.

My mother, Esther, was raised in Unadilla, New York — a small, upstate town. She was raised Christian, but my father was an atheist. That made it difficult to know who to follow when I was growing up.

The day that my mother and father married they left New York City on promises of work in California framing houses. However, when they got there the promised work was non-existent. So they headed back to New York. While driving, they came across the southern states and ended up in Odessa, Texas. They stayed six months — long enough to have their first child, Roy, born in 1952.

## Fort Worth beginnings

After Roy was born, my parents moved to Fort Worth and never left the area. So I was born a Fort Worth Texan. Then they filled out the rest of our family with one child after another, until there were five. My father kept my mother barefoot and pregnant; she never drove a car until I was a teenager. That was my father's way of keeping her at home and clear of his many extramarital affairs.

I was born while they lived in a duplex on Maurice Street. By the time we left there, the family of five children was complete. Seven of us lived in a small duplex in probably less than 600 square feet.

We moved to 5045 Monna Court, my parents' first experience in home ownership. It was about 1,000 square feet and we lived there until I was a teenager. My father did all kinds of things to make a living such as selling life insurance, trading his time for dollars. He eventually decided to get into the security patrol business and ended up buying a car on credit in Haltom City, a suburb of Fort Worth. For a fee of $10 or $15 a month he would check on different businesses at night. He drove all night long to make sure doors were locked, appropriate lights were on, and no employees or burglars were breaking in.

Through that process, he got acquainted with car dealers by checking on their businesses. Over time, he became friends with some of them. He checked their doors at night, made sure all the keys to the cars were put up and not left inside the vehicles, made sure the cars weren't messed with by people trying to take tires and wheels off.

My father received most of his income through that security patrol service — up to $600 a month —and that's what we lived on. The dealers kept telling him that if he wanted to feed his family of seven, he'd have to do more than that.

They suggested that maybe he should get into the car business. A few of them volunteered that if my father got into financing used cars, they'd take some of their old, beat-up junker cars that were too rough for their customers and give them to him free of charge and help him out in any way they could.

Well, it took a while but he decided he should give it a shot.

Even though I grew up in a tight family and a close-knit neighborhood, and had a lot of fun while we lived in Haltom City, I learned to have a great hatred for poverty because my mother and father fought all the time over lack of money. We had second, third, and fourth hand-me-downs. There never was more than enough food in the house. At times, we ate cereal with a fork so that we could pass the milk to the next kid. Poverty was a constant. I identified it as an unacceptable way of life; I didn't like it and wanted to change that in my life.

## Lot Rat beginnings and adventures

When we were "old enough," my siblings and I started working with my father. I was about 10 years old. He'd take us with him on night patrol. We'd shake the doors and check them, walk with him in the dark, and check for burglars.

As I said, although he had horrible morals, my father instilled a great work ethic in us. During the time that he worked security patrol and met car dealers, my father also worked closely with the Haltom City police force. As a child I sometimes freaked out because every now and then police officers would be in front of our house and I couldn't figure out why. Because of the dysfunction at home, I thought my father was a bad guy because of that. But he wasn't.

In addition to his security job as night patrol, my father started a repossession business. I remember in the early days of my life watching him do some really strange things. I didn't realize at the time that he was repossessing vehicles, but he and whomever else he was working with were always out at night. Car dealers wanted him to help locate vehicles because he was out anyway.

My father and the people he worked with would take long, thick nylon ropes and attach metal hooks to each end. He wrapped the metal hooks with duct tape so that when they were put onto bumpers they wouldn't make any noise. Eventually he took my brothers and me out at night when we were not even teenagers yet. We would go riding along while he and his crew repossessed cars. That was kind of a freaky thing.

That was also my first exposure to buy-here pay-here.

When I was about 10 years old, the phone numbers in our area weren't strictly numbers. They began with names like Edison or Terminal or Watson and that was the lead of the phone number. Ours was TE4-0700; we were instructed never to answer the phone at home and I didn't understand why — I thought it was really odd.

But I noticed my mother would answer the phone with her sweet voice and talk quietly. She always answered and said, "TE4-0700." Well, that seemed strange. The next thing I knew she would take notes.

Later I learned that she took notes from car dealers about information regarding future repossessions. One day, I thought, *I wanna answer that phone, I can do that.* So I entered my first real-life exposure to the repo business besides the duct-taped ropes and pulling cars. There was somebody on the other end of the phone who wanted to give information.

Because I had a child's voice, I sounded like a female. The man on the other end said, "Mrs. Carlson?" and I said, "Yes." He told me he wanted to give me some information about cars that he needed to have repossessed. When he spoke I didn't clearly understand all that he was saying. Well, I wrote down terrible, terrible notes, and when my father came home and found out what I had done, man I was berated — it was horrible. But that phone call was my first introduction to the buy-here pay-here business and left me wondering what that was all about. It created a curiosity in me.

## The other family business begins

Around 1965, my father had been seriously kicking around an idea to move us all to Arkansas, buy land, plant pecan trees and go into business farming pecans.

I don't know why, and I don't know what the arrangements were because I know he didn't have any money. But my father went into a partnership with somebody instead of moving us to Arkansas. I was relieved. I didn't want to be uprooted.

He and his partner opened a used-car lot on Riverside Drive in the poor part of town. He shared some cars with other dealers and I don't know how they got that worked out. He was still doing repossession work on the side along with the night patrol. Well, he got overloaded and couldn't handle everything. By the middle of 1966, he bailed out of Riverside Drive. So he failed at his first attempt.

But he tried again in 1969 and went to a bank to try to borrow $500. They told him, "Mr. Carlson, you can't afford to pay it back. We can't loan you the money." So my father took what little bit of furniture he had and decided to leverage that. He got the loan on his furniture and used that money to buy two Rambler station wagons. I remember them very distinctly. One was standard shift. One was beige. The other was seafoam green. We had to paint them both and do some mechanical work. One cost us $175 wholesale, the other cost $225. I don't know how we survived with such a meager amount of capital, but we did.

Sometime shortly after a debacle with the company's first skip when a guy bought one of those cars and took off for Walla Walla Washington, my father sat me down and explained his goal to me. He wanted to be sure that I understood his goal. He said that if he could just get to $1,800 a month income, he would be set for life. He wanted me to know that number. However when he died in the spring of 1989, he left an $8 million estate.

# CHAPTER TWO:

## From Lot Rat to Sales at Age 16

During the time that my father was a partner on Riverside Drive, I became one of his lot rats. The dealership sold old cars that were built in the 1950s. For whatever reason, people didn't keep their cars clean back then. When my father and partner bought them, they were in horrible, horrible dirty condition. They would get them for $150, $175, $200.

We, his sons, had the job after school and during summers to clean the cars — not only the ones that came in to be cleaned up, but to keep the already cleaned ones on the lot in top shape.

Keep in mind that we were teenage boys. We worked in a lean-to in the summertime without air conditioning and without heat in the winter on a shingle tab lot. When it rained it was muddy. We spent hot days after school and summers cleaning those nasty, stinking cars. We vacuumed them and applied polish by hand. Some had really bad paint jobs because clear coat protective coatings weren't used then. They were all horrible paint jobs. On many we had to use compound and buffer pads.

My brothers and I had soap and grime all over us when we washed the cars, and used water hoses, not even high-pressure hoses. You know young teenagers, we sprayed each other for laughs; but the job was miserable, it was horrible. Especially living in Texas with 100 plus degree days with virtually no shade except for that lean-to with stinking, nasty cars. I hated it.

We did that all day long. On Saturdays we'd start at about 8 o'clock in the morning, but we wouldn't get home until 10 o'clock that night. We would have been cleaning cars or just hanging around the lot the whole time.

We'd go home to our small, wood-frame house and take a bath without changing out the water. By the time the fourth boy was finished, the bathwater was black, every night.

People made fun of us. Our neighbors taunted us and said that their parents said that we were going to go broke in that business, not ever get paid, and that our father was working us like slaves. Just laughing, laughing, laughing.

That's a good example of when I talk about being an entrepreneur — you gotta put blinders on and not pay attention to those things.

So yeah, I was a lot rat. It was horrible. I wouldn't want to go back through it — but it was good that I did at the time because it was a place to start. It made me appreciate the people who own and run those businesses. It is not something I recommend as a way to get started, but it was necessary for us at the time.

But it made me hate cars. My mother was educated as a nurse, but only practiced a short time because my father kept her barefoot and pregnant. She wanted me to be a doctor. I had geared all of my schooling in that direction; I wanted to be a doctor — NOT a car guy. I've grown to like finance and the analytical world of finance. But I still don't like cars.

## My first sale and my first skip

When I was still underage and my father had gone into the car business again after 1969, he "hired" me to work the family business with him. But he clearly instructed me, "Do not sell a car" when he was away from the lot. I could take down information, but not sell a car.

Well, I didn't heed that warning.

I figured that I'd seen him do what he does, and knew I could do that.

A woman came in, asking about a car. I told her that I would take her credit application, which I was instructed not to do, but not forbidden. My father had always told me that if I ever wanted to take a credit app I had to fill in every blank, don't leave anything empty.

So while he was away from the lot one day, I took that responsibility and filled it all out — I got every question answered in detail. I thought, *Well, I'm confident with this and I know how to sell the car. I know the price and I can just pick out another contract that was sold at the same price. I can fill it out and match that and change the dates.*

So I did that and I delivered a 1964 Chevrolet Biscayne to the woman.

Later, my father came back and the first thing he said was, "Where's that Chevrolet? Where's that Biscayne?" And I said, "I sold it." I was happy. I was gloating. I thought, *I'll show you I can do this.*

He wasn't so impressed. He said, "Get me that credit app." I showed it to him. He looked through it, scanning quickly and said, "We will never find this car, ever!"

I said, "How can you say that?"

He said, "Because none of these addresses are real."

Well, he knew that from all the repo work he'd done. He said the Social Security number wasn't real and that we'd never find this person. Sure enough, we never found her. It was my first sale and my first skip.

The lesson that I learned was that not only did I have to fill out all the blanks of a credit application; I had to get the right information and verify it.

Where a lot of dealers fail is that they get information — a lot of times not all the information — and then they fail to verify. I learned a very valuable lesson. But I was in good company — my father's first sale skipped to Walla Walla, and he had all the experience.

I worked for my father from 1969 until I graduated from high school in 1971 at age 17. That was when the draft was going on with the Vietnam War, and I was inducted. I went to my physical. At the end, we're all standing there naked, and the doctor says to me, "Son, do you know of any reason why you can't join the military?" I said, "Well, I think I should tell you that when I was a kid, about 11 years old, I dove off a dock in a public swimming pool. I arched my back really bad because I saw the bottom coming up, opened my eyes at the last minute, and my back legs came over to the top of my head. I cracked my back really bad on the pool bottom and it nearly knocked me out. Ever since then I've had problems with my lower back. At the time I had numbness going down the front of my legs and my two middle toes, and would alternate between my right leg and left leg at different times." He hollered, "Son, you're outta here!" as he slammed his 4F stamp down onto my paperwork.

The significance of this incident is that I was second in birth order and my older brother Roy opted to join the Navy. Because he was to be gone for four years, I was moved to number one position to learn the car business. I grabbed that with all the gusto I could. I think that was a break for me.

# CHAPTER THREE:

## Learning the Ropes without Duct Tape

It took much effort from my father and his four sons, three years and a lot of help from other people and businesses like the wrecker company we used before we saw any real progress.

The guy, Fred Morris who owned a wrecker service, would let us go a year without paying him for wrecker pulls. He said, "Just pay me when you can, I know you'll eventually be big, just pay me when you can."

For years, anytime Carlson family members had a wrecker issue, Fred would do the work for free, no matter what. He was a great guy. Car dealers and other vendors helped us; they understood what we wanted to do and they wanted our family to succeed. That's human interest. They helped us, and that is one big reason why I like to help people.

My father had a friend named LD Hardwick. LD was having struggles with a guy who worked for him who wasn't very kind. LD was in his 60s and had befriended my father.

His business was on East Lancaster Avenue; our first location was on Rosedale Street. LD had an opportunity to buy another location from another dealer who was going out of business because he had decided to retire and sell out. So LD bought the location and offered to rent it to my father for $300 so we could open our second location on East Lancaster. My father was willing to take that on.

We immediately started putting cars on Lancaster Avenue. When we were solely on Rosedale, it took us three years of working our tails off to get to 100 active accounts paying us $10 and $15 dollars per week. But when we moved to East Lancaster, almost overnight we grew to 200 accounts. I don't know how that happened so quickly, but it did.

We also learned lessons from other car dealers. There was one dealer in particular who had about 800 active accounts but we only had 100. Bobby Sides got acquainted with my father and taught him a huge lesson that we didn't know about — how to use "float."

We could issue a draft, and whoever we bought the vehicle from had to wait until they had the title and all documents associated with the vehicle assigned to our company before they could get paid. It got put through their bank. Their bank sent it to our bank, and thus we benefitted from holding onto our cash longer as a "float." Sometimes that float would be two weeks or more. That float was part of what enabled us to jump up to the next 200 accounts within the next six months.

Then about six months in business at our new location, LD's health started to fail after he had bought out the older man's business. Along with his health failing, LD found out that the guy who worked for him was not doing the right things by him. LD's wife was also having health issues, so he decided to sell all of his notes in bulk. I'd never heard of that.

That was my first exposure with anybody having an asset or a note that could be sold for cash. It stuck inside my head. I thought, *Well that's an interesting business.*

So LD sold his accounts, got good money for them, and then came to my father and said, "Look, why don't you take over this location too? Shut down your Rosedale lot."

Overwhelmed by LD's proposition, my father said, "I can't afford to take that big lot on. I can't afford to put the cars on it."

But LD said, "I'll let you have the inventory on my lot." It was probably about 50 cars. He told my father that he could pay for them 12 months later free of any interest charge.

What a break that was. So we sold them, got down payments and regular payments, and bought even more vehicles. That year of selling and reselling those 50 cars gave us the ability to succeed on an even greater scale. In about 18 months we were at 500 active, paying accounts. When a business like ours gets to 500 accounts, it's really clicking. That is an organization.

We started opening more locations. By the time I'd put in about 10 years, I became the Chief Operations Officer. At that point I was responsible for everything except legal, accounting, and banking. My father handled those things; I handled everything else.

By the time I left almost 20 years later, we had financed roughly 35,000 cars. I officially started in 1969 and left the family business in 1988. We had never sold off an account.

# CHAPTER FOUR:

## Indirect Lending Almost Got the Best of Me

There is one incident that stands out which brought me to the mindset that I wanted to get out of the used-car lot business and try my hand at indirect lending.

One beautiful day around springtime as I stood in the car lot with my hands planted on my hips, I looked around at all the people milling around. There were so many, the car lot looked like a moving cornfield. At that time I was in charge of all operations — everything. One of our facilities held about 175 cars in inventory. I was thinking, *We cannot afford to sell all these cars. We just can't.*

I was also thinking about how we had just a down payment, there was all that money on the street, but we had to wait to get it. And I said to myself, *We just can't do it.*

Then a thought stuck inside my head. I wished that there was a mechanism to let us simply keep the down payments and give up the receivables and move on so we could sell more cars without running out of money.

My thoughts continued. I thought of how big and financially strong our business was. If that could work for us — and I would like that — surely smaller dealers would like that. I thought, *There's probably a business in that. Someday we need to do that.* That's when my first inkling of point-of-sale indirect lending came up.

My father received mixed life lessons from his parents who were immigrants. He was taught by his father that, "You can't make money by borrowing money." His mother said, "You must borrow money to make money."

So because of his lack of respect for his mother and his respect for his father, he resisted with great tenacity the idea of borrowing money. I kicked him in the tail for about seven years to borrow money. We had plenty sitting in the bank and in savings accounts and he just wouldn't use it. I finally convinced him to borrow against his own money, so we borrowed at a rate of like half a point over what the bank paid us on our money — we borrowed $1 million.

After we did that, our profits went through the roof. It just made us really take off. I told my father that under no circumstances were we going to pay that money back. He was not to get anxious about it and pay it back — just keep it out there, don't ever pay it back.

We didn't have it as a term loan. It was just a line of credit in which we were required only to pay accruing interest. I wanted to use it for 10 years.

Well, my father paid it off in about two and a half years because he just couldn't stand owing the money. About a year later he said, "Man, borrowing that million dollars just made a tremendous difference, didn't it?" I said, "Yeah, it made a lot of difference."

We learned from that.

I saw the potential of making serious money in the buy-here pay-here business.

## From lot rat to billionaire dreams

Because I hated poverty so desperately, I focused on studying wealthy people. I decided that I was going to become a billionaire.

I studied the Bass family in Fort Worth. The Basses inherited $50 million from Sid Richardson Bass who made a lot of money in oil and gas. They decided as a family that instead of dividing that money up, they would keep it together in one place. Because they kept it together, it had more power. They eventually went into investment banking and became billionaires.

So I decided that if I could just get to $50 million or $100 million in net worth and then get into investment banking, then that would be my life's passion. That's what I'd want to do, and I wanted to become a billionaire. Admittedly, it was for sick reasons that I wanted to. At the time, I thought it was something everybody should want to do.

When I left the family business in 1988 we had financed 35,000 cars. We had five locations and more than 50 employees, and I was in charge of all of it. I don't tell this story to brag. There is a lesson here about what all I should have learned then, if I was paying attention.

My father paid me well. At that time from 1986-1988, he paid me over $200,000 a year, all things considered. Ultimately, he and I became strained with each other because he had promised that we would continue growing the company, but I had already pushed him way past his comfort zone. He had small-town mentality. He wanted to put the brakes on. Out of his anger, he offered to sell me the company for $5 million.

I asked, "Do I need to get that in writing?"

He said, "No, just shake my hand."

I thought, *Well, he's my father, I'll just shake his hand.* So I did and then immediately made a phone call to Clifton Morris who was the co-founder of Urcarco which eventually became AmeriCredit in Fort Worth. Urcarco had been trying to get my dad to sell to them.

Clifton answered the phone and I said, "Hey Cliff, here's the deal. My father won't sell his company to you, but he will sell it to me. I don't think he comprehends the current value of our company. I think its worth about $10 million. He thinks it's worth about $5 million. Will you loan me the money to buy the company subject to merger, and then we'll make our other trade on the excess value in stock?"

Clifton asked about cash flow, receivables, inventory, and things like that before he agreed that my father's business was probably worth about $10 million. He told me to go back and do the trade and get back with him. Due diligence, I get that.

So my father gave me permission to talk with my brothers. Long story short, when it came down to the harsh, cold reality of selling to me and my siblings, when I let my father know that I had tentatively lined up the money, he exploded.

I was so at odds with him at that point that he basically told me that he already paid me enough money and that from now on, when he told me to jump; I was to ask him, "How high?"

I couldn't live with that. So I exited the company. It was scary and exciting at the same time.

What happened next took us all completely by surprise — we didn't see it coming. On July 1, 1988 my mother died. My father died less than a year later in the spring of 1989 and had not done any estate planning. He had a will, but it passed everything to the five of us equally and undivided. But, because both of our parents died without proper estate planning, everything was double-taxed and almost taxed us out of business.

That's another danger for car dealers; if they don't take care of estate planning and everything else, they could lose it all. We almost did. We had to sell off our parents' 200-acre ranch home, 440 dairy acres they owned, other income properties and car lots, and the banks called the credit line. It was a huge disaster. We barely made it out of the mess he left for us to clean up. But we did eventually turn it around.

## Trial and error looking for partners

At the time that I left working for my father, I committed all of my net worth to pursue the idea of indirect lending. I just knew it would work.

But I had to overcome the fact that I was a shy young man.

Because of my upbringing I had a lot of fear about a lot of things in the world around me. I also didn't have the benefit of going to college. I felt like I was under-educated even though I managed to go through and survive the school of hard knocks growing up on car lots with a demanding, verbally abusive father who ruled with an iron fist.

Even at age 19 when I was in charge at the front desk, I looked even younger than I was and customers thought I was too young to be in charge.

As I aged, I still fought those battles and went through the learning curves of how to hire and fire people, how to assess my own efforts, how to run a business when I hadn't been trained professionally. I had to figure it all out on my own through trial and error.

In my case, I had a dominating father who tried to put his ideas into my head and hold me accountable. That was challenging. When I came of age and ran the family buy-here pay-here business, I had about 2,500 active accounts, about 60 employees, and was responsible for all operations with the exception of banking, legal, and accounting.

Then I had to deal with the hurdles of working. I worked eight years without a vacation, 12 hours a day, six days a week. That was something I had to overcome and realize that I didn't have to do that to be in business.

Another hurdle was trying to break away from my father when the pressure just became too much. I had to make a decision about which business to go into if I went into another one. I had never started one myself, so I needed to figure out how to go about that.

It was daunting for me when I decided to be in the indirect lending business and pulled pieces together such as finding attorneys, accountants, partners, and put together business plans without ever having done that. Then I had to learn how to go out and talk to owners of dealerships. In the late 1980s, the indirect lending business was a brand new concept.

At that time, dealerships sold receivables in bulk, and the idea of selling point-of-sale was just getting started. I learned how to communicate with people who had money to be potential partners, and get them to understand my industry, and that even though it looked like there was a lot of risk, properly measured and controlled, it could be very profitable.

It was only because I already had 20 years of experience in the industry and originated over 35,000 loans during that period that I was able to get the attention of investors and partners. Once I gained partners, I needed to figure out how to keep them from trying to take control, take everything, and squeeze me down to nothing. I had to go through that struggle.

I went through the high level college of business without going to college. I learned about asset securitizations and lockbox agents and trust agreements and high-level corporate stuff that I never imagined myself being involved in.

After three years into modeling indirect lending and actually doing business and generating receivables, I proved that up and attracted partners.

One potential associate that I negotiated a deal with was Richard Rainwater. He recently died with a net worth of about $3 billion. At the time, his net worth was about $300 million.

Anyway, he made his money working with the Basses of Fort Worth. Somehow a stroke of luck got me into his office. Turned out that it wasn't actually Richard that was going to be my partner, but John Goff who worked with him. (By now, he's probably billionaire status.) John told me they were going to put up $3 million in equity, and that they would allow me to keep controlling interest of the company, but they required leverage from the banks.

Turned out the banks wouldn't loan the money for our start-up without Richard putting up $5 million dollars. So I wasn't able to get that deal done.

Another potential partnership who came to my table were Tom Greg and Ted Torro. They wanted to get $3 million dollars from an entity called Spear Leeds & Kellog. They were willing to invest $3 million, but that was subject to our company securing a $12 million line of credit from Glenfed Financial Corporation. Our agreement was that I was going to have control of the company as well.

Well, they sent someone down from up north to close the deal. The guy who was supposed to close the deal took me out to dinner — and then stomped on me verbally at the end of the meal like I was a little kid in trouble.

He told me he was going to sue me to death if I tried to screw him out of his money. It freaked me out so bad. I thought, *Oh my gosh, do I really want to do business with them?* But I was willing to do it anyway.

The next day, Ted Torro and Tom Greg said, "Okay, we're going to squeeze you down below 50 percent." I was not about to give up control of my company to anyone who would treat me like my father had in the past. I walked away from that deal.

Ted and Tom went off to do business on their own even though they had signed non-disclosure agreements with me. However, before they left, they asked what name I would have used if I hadn't chosen AutoCredit as a company name. I told them my secondary name was Vehicle Acceptance Corporation.

Well, they created Vehicle Acceptance Corporation which still exists today out of Dallas. They found someone in the check-cashing business, and got him to partner with them based on the education that I had given them. So much for our non-disclosure agreements. They ended up selling out their interest to another entity which is the Vehicle Acceptance Corporation that has gone on and succeeded to this day.

The other potential partner I had was a guy named Charlie Bradley. His team came to the table and was going to put up $3 million, and I was going to have control.

But someone from my office spooked them when we were at the redline stage and ready to close within a day or two. They walked away.

Again with the education I had given them, a potential partner went out and found another prospect in California. They partnered with an entity and became Consumer Portfolio Services which has generated about $9 billion in receivables.

I did manage to find true partners in the end. We eventually raised $100 million in assets and equity offerings to build our business.

Additionally, we were the first company ever in America to raise money with public debt but without insurance. Nothing was insured, there wasn't a rating agency involved. Nobody had ever done that, yet we went on to do it.

We took my company public in 1993 via of a reverse triangular merger with a cleaned up NOL public shell Search Natural Resources which we eventually renamed Search Financial Services. At our peak in Spring of 1994, we were processing 6,000 loans per month and closing on 2,000, which was costing us approximately $12 million a month in new funding through securitization.

But the securitization market shifted on us. We made some fatal business mistakes and missed our earnings and couldn't secure funds like we had been doing.

It was a disaster. Now there was pressure from investors filing lawsuits, crashing my company and attempts to take everything I ever dreamed. The whole company came crashing down. It went from being a $200 million-plus NASDAQ market cap company with over 200 employees to a total nightmare. I hung in there until early 1996 fighting for our survival.

Search Financial Services got out of indirect lending to the low-end of substandard credit. We moved up into the higher end of credit, functioning more like an AmeriCredit company, and I started learning about proper credit evaluations through analysis with credit agencies. I learned about regression analysis, many other methods of statistical analysis and scoring which eventually led to AutoZoom years later.

We then hired a team of three guys: George C. Evans, Anthony J. Dellavechia, and James F. Leary, whose claim-to-fame was growing Associates Financial Services from $3 million in earnings to $100 million in earnings. We ended up opening over 30 consumer branches of Search Financial Services that were direct lending offices.

George Evans knocked on Search's office door one day when we lived in Dallas. He had heard about our tragic story. He said, "Hey, I'll turn this around for you." So we hired him immediately to do that. That's why we had so many consumer branches.

In the end, we couldn't clean up all of the mess that we faced; the damage was too deep. We ended up selling the whole heap off to Blazer Financial and got out by the skin of our teeth.

My high level of success had come crashing down around me. I had to hang in there for an additional three or four years until I got unwound from it. That was very trying. Afterwards, I spent five years re-grouping and did not do much of anything related to used-car finance until I could get my head back on straight.

# CHAPTER FIVE:

## The Turnaround to AutoZoom

Wives go kind of nuts when husbands take a five-year break from working and bringing in a steady paycheck.

My wife, Carroll Ann, eventually kicked me hard enough that I finally had to go do something about it before we ran completely out of money.

I decided I was going to re-create a new indirect lending company. Allen Dobbins of AutoStar and I are friends, and he had sold me our software that we had used before in the other indirect lending business.

One day I said, "Hey, let's create an indirect lending company together. We'll platform off of your dealer base and your technology knowledge along with my financial knowledge and ability to raise money."

So we put together a package to go do that. We solicited investors and tentatively had some money circled up to launch our business. That was in 2001. Then the Twin

Towers got hit and everything was over. Nobody could get a penny from anybody for anything.

By then my wife was really freaking out. So I thought, *Well, what am I going to do now?*

I started dealer consulting. Through that consulting, I determined that the primary challenge that every dealer faces is finding a way to standardize their underwriting and their decision-making processes.

So I asked myself, *How do we remove ourselves from the equation of "decisioning" without losing control? How do we measure and monitor to make sure the people that we train are not deviating from what we've taught them? And how do we take comfort in any of that?*

I determined that there was a need for this solution. I partnered with Allen Dobbins and a few other friends. We created Auto Loan Technologies, LLC (AutoZoom) in 2002.

So, that is how I got back into the used-car finance industry. I started meeting with car dealers locally and then around the country, determining that there was a need that wasn't being fulfilled. I identified that need and filled it, and built scoring solutions, which I've been doing for a long time now as AutoZoom.

It could be said that believing one could possibly become a billionaire is like chasing unicorns and rainbows. During the darkest years, the most important, life changing lesson that I ever learned came.

What I found was that in the total disaster of losing my dream to become a billionaire, Christ found me where I was, as low as snail slime on the floor. He found me in that and placed in me a peace and joy for life that I had never known. And He instilled in me a passion for people. He helped me to realize that all I need is Him. I didn't need ink on paper to be a billionaire.

I'm a Christian. One of the things I've learned about myself and the way I live my life is that I have a passion for people. Not only do I have a passion and a heart to have a positive impact in people's lives, I enjoy helping people make more money and improve their businesses and even get out of financial trouble — to enhance some way financially. I have a great passion for that, and that is what drives me.

# CHAPTER SIX:

# A Fax Machine Taught Me to Be Open

One of the first lessons I learned back in the days when I worked for my father was to be open to new ideas so they wouldn't potentially come back and bite me.

The guys in the buy-here pay-here industry will understand this concept: imagine having all the employees that I had with the accounts I managed and the pressures and phone lines and being the end-of-the-line guy for all the tragedies and problems in the business, when some vendor calls on me and wants to share some new something that she thought would be great for us.

I didn't really give vendors a lot of time.

The incident that made me change my mind was when a lady came by who worked with a typewriter supply company out of Fort Worth. She insisted that it would be beneficial for me to use a new thing called a facsimile machine, also called a fax machine.

She was comfortable coming into my office because she'd always sold us our adding machines and calculators. She was excited to tell me about these new fax machines. She had pamphlets with her. She tried to explain to me what fax machines are and how they work, but I was busy like most every car dealer — was so busy. (Many dealers don't slow down to listen to what vendors have to say — just like some dealers don't listen to anything about AutoZoom. You're telling them what it can do for them and they're just not open.) Well I wasn't open to fax machines because it was a new technology and didn't make sense.

The salesperson couldn't satisfactorily explain a fax machine. I finally asked her to just leave a brochure. When she walked out the door, I threw it in the trash. I wasn't going to mess with that. When she came back on another visit later, I put her off and told her to come back when she could tell me more about it.

Well, she was persistent. She came back and said, "I know more about it now, let me tell you about them." She gave me different brochures. She said, "You see that piece of paper right there with that writing on it? That printing on it? You can lie that on this machine, put it under this, close the lid, and send it from one over there," and she pointed to my office, "and you can send it to this other one."

And I thought, *This lady is an idiot. I am not that lazy. I'll copy it and carry it. I don't have to do that.* Brilliant, right? Well, I threw the brochures away again.

Later realized what a big mistake I'd made. From then on, it stuck in my mind that I had made an error by not listening to that girl. I didn't slow down to listen to her. I thought about how if somebody wanted to get in the indirect lending business and buy paper from other dealers, this is how I would do it. And it stuck.

My wake-up call was many months later when my sales rep, Reba Blevens with WBAP radio suggested that I fly with helicopter pilot and traffic reporter Dick Siegel. We did a lot of advertising with them. Reba said that when I was done flying, they'd drop me off at the station and she would show me around.

Well, I went. After they dropped me off we're walking through the station and all of a sudden I hear this weird warble. I said, "What is *that*?" I'd never heard it before. Reba said, "Oh, that's a fax machine." Well I'd heard of that. I asked what it did. As we walked over I could see thermal paper peeling off of it. She said, "Watch."

A news update came across, and I said, "Wow! What office did that come from?" I was looking around at the internal offices and she said, "Dallas." There we were in Fort Worth about 35 miles away. I mentally just hit myself in the head and thought, *Boy, you're an idiot.*

I immediately went back to my office and asked the typewriter supply people to get me all the information I needed about getting fax machines. Turns out, it was going to cost about $1,000 each at the time, and we needed about seven.

I took the information to my father and said, "Hey, we need this."

One issue that buy-here pay-here dealers have to deal with is that underwriting needs to be centralized. If there are multiple locations, centralizing gives better control. And I saw the benefit instantly — fax machines would give us great control.

But my father said, "We're not going to spend $7,000 for these." He was real crusty. I was so upset. But that put a trigger inside my head that went, *This is how you buy paper from other dealers. This is the mechanism.* We needed the paper to come to us centrally through fax machines. That was another genesis toward indirect lending.

## The seed is planted

I used that idea to build my indirect lending company.

I was closed-minded before, but eventually became open through that experience. It could have bypassed me altogether, and if it had, I might not have ever gotten into the indirect lending business.

I've seen dealers at conventions who walk right by booths as if they have blinders on. I don't know that they're not open. It might be that they have preconceived ideas about knowing what those products are. They think, *Oh, I know what that is. I'm not interested in that.*

For example, when I first approached my family about using AutoZoom for our family business, Mike Carlson Motor Company, and creating a scoring model for them and scored values to go by, one of the first questions they asked is, "How in the world are you going to help us make a decision about a buy-here pay-here customer with a single score? That just doesn't make sense to us."

They were confused. They had drawn the conclusion that it was not possible to make a decision about credit worthiness or what to do with a customer based upon a single number when they had been making all their decisions with their gut and feel and by basic guidelines. To deviate from that was scary. So by the conclusion they drew that it couldn't be possible, they weren't open. Only because I was family was I able to get them to open their minds and try it. They were among the first 100 who signed up.

Some people are just closed about a topic. Some people are afraid. Humans mostly have a fear of the unknown. If they're already comfortable with what's working and they have fears about trying something new, they're most likely not going to be brave enough to ask questions that lead to change.

A lot of times I find that buy-here pay-here dealers are guys or girls who got started in the businesses by accident — maybe they didn't fit well in other parts of the world, trading time for dollars or didn't like having bosses. For whatever reason, they stumbled into the industry. Then they become very successful in buy-here, pay-here. They are self-made. They might be afraid to ask questions or afraid to show any weakness and let you know that they're not as informed about something. That will keep them from being open. That is true not only for buy-here pay-here people, but business people in general.

A lot of times people will settle for what is enough to just get them by because they are comfortable with what they know. It's easier to stay there rather than be open to looking at what they're afraid of and being uncomfortable with the unknown.

# CHAPTER SEVEN:

# Persistence Paid Off

A t one point when I first started out, I founded an indirect lending company called AutoCredit. Eventually we rolled it into a public shell out of Dallas, Texas.

A team of partners and I determined that we were going to raise money through asset securitizations. We were not willing to take serious dilution of ownership equity in our company. So, we decided to raise money through asset securitizations rather than equity offerings and to not take money from friends and family even in those securitizations or private placements of debt. We were going to raise money through a network of securities broker dealers. If we couldn't raise it through broker dealers, then we just weren't going to do the business.

That took a tremendous amount of persistence. Our first million-dollar private placement that we put on the street paid an 18 percent coupon to investors. It was a three-year investment, and we paid a 10 percent front-end load —

printing cost, legal fees, commissions — so it was a very expensive way to raise money. Even with it having that high rate of return to investors, there was a lot of fear involved on the investor's part when we first got started.

The broker dealers didn't quite understand how the investment was safe. So we worked for six months just to raise the first $300,000 which is what it took to break escrow before we could claim success, shut that fund down, and go to the next one.

We did cross that threshold in six months — it almost broke us to wait that long — but we did cross the threshold, claimed success, and shut down that fund. By then we had a lot of momentum-interested prospective investors. When we claimed success on that, we raised another million almost immediately with a lower rate, better terms and better things for us, because of that momentum through the broker-dealer network.

We continued to do that and raised a total of $4.3 million in private placements. Then one of our attorneys came to us and said, "We've got a problem."

I said, "Wait a minute, what do you mean, 'We've got a problem?'"

He said, "We've hit what's called an integration problem."

"What do you mean an integration problem? I don't know what you're talking about."

Well, when you raise money in private placements like this and accept money from a certain number of non-accredited investors, once you raise $5 million, you have to shut down that effort for six months and give it a break before you can continue that same methodology.

"Well, we can't stop," I said. "What's the option?"

"You can do a public debt deal."

"Great, let's go do that."

"That requires you have insurance. You have to insure the investment."

"Great, we'll go do that. How do we do that?"

"Well, you've gotta get a rating agency to rate the transaction."

"Great, we've got a relationship with Fireman's Fund for insurance."

We met with Fireman's Fund and they told us that they would love to quote pricing and do business with us but we needed to go to Duff & Phelps, Standard and Poor's, and Moody's rating agencies to get a rating on our investment vehicle.

So we met with all of those rating agencies. They all came back to us and said that they couldn't rate our transaction because we had a repo rate in excess of 40 percent.

I said, "So what? Look at the returns after losses. We have a much better return after losses than GM, Ford, and Chrysler."

The powers that be said that it didn't matter; we had a 40 percent repo rate, and they could not rate our transactions.

So we met with other insurance companies. Their people said that they would love to insure our investment but couldn't without a rating agency.

Well, gosh. Were we just dead in the water? We couldn't stop there. It was crazy.

So we kept pressing the law firm, "What's our option?" We didn't give up. We were persistent. I kept saying, "No, we can't stop. We gotta raise the money."

Finally someone told us that our only option was to do a public debt deal, but without insurance, it's never been done.

I said, "Okay," and asked if there was anything else to prevent us from doing it or trying it. They said, "No," but that it could prove to be very expensive because it was probably going to cost us about half a million dollars in legal accounting, printing, and getting past all the blue sky regulations and everything. Even then we could spend the half a million and still not be able to raise a nickel because the investment community out there is accustomed to insured deals.

So we got together as partners and decided to do the deal because we had the capital. It took us six months.

That took persistence, not knowing if we were going to succeed. But we had so much momentum through the broker-dealer network, once we put that offering out that we had $5 million raised, it took hardly any time.

We had so much more momentum that we raised another $10 million, and then $15 million, and then we decided to take the company public and did a secondary public stock offering because it was an NOL (net operating loss) shell roll up and we sold off 20 percent of the company in common stock for $23 million.

Right behind that we did a $20 million public debt offering. Then we worked out a trade with a very large regional brokerage firm for four individual $100 million private placements to fund our business, subject to things continuing to be in good shape.

We raised money through broker dealers and proved that we could do it our way. It was a zoo and a nightmare, and it took a lot of persistence on our side.

## Consistency is key

The important thing about being consistent is to be dependable in your efforts, to be high integrity, to do what you say you're going to do when you say you're going to do it.

One way to ensure consistency is to under-promise and over-deliver in every case that you can. You can't always hit the target, but at least be consistent about making an effort to get there.

And consistently remember that you're serving others. You don't get business that lasts with anyone without being consistently high-integrity and providing something that's worthwhile.

That's what the Lord put us here for. We're here to serve others.

# CHAPTER EIGHT:

## Systems-Driven vs Personality-Driven

A lot of businesses are personality-driven. For example, mom and pop decide to open a hamburger stand, ice cream shop, or anything like that. Instead of being a business built around technologies, they have hands-on procedures.

In comparison, McDonald's has systems. There are automated systems such as keeping food temperatures at the correct levels.

There were thousands of hamburger stands across the United States before McDonald's took off in 1955 and created their franchises — which are systems-driven.

The whole franchise thing has become systems-driven not only with food services, but with many other products.

Technologies can be systems-driven. For example, the buy-here, pay-here business is more systems-driven now, whereas when my family first got started, everything we did was manual. There were no computers, no software. We took payments from customers and recorded those payments on three-by-five cards, not even the pre-lined kind. We actually lined them with a ruler ourselves and tracked the payment. Then we wrote by hand into a hand ledger — and boy that was impossible to keep balanced.

Eventually our accountants suggested that we use what the doctors use. It was a One Write system — or what they called a pegboard system. There was a complicated mess of carbon copy stuff we had to put down on a ledger, then put down a carbon, then a ledger card, then another carbon, then a receipt over the top of that. We wrote on the receipt, then the receipt posted to the customer's individual ledger card, then posted to the general ledger. It became a system. It saved us a lot of accounting time, but man, did our people resist it! They cried and moaned because it was different.

Although it was manual, it was still systems-driven and it saved us a lot of time and effort in accounting. We became consistent and reliable in our accounting, and our lenders liked that better. Our accountants liked it because it was easier to file our taxes.

Another example for the benefits of being systems-driven are the Dealership Management Systems (DMS) systems, the 50 or 60 software companies that all used-car dealers are dependent upon to accurately track inventory and properly compute contracts and manage collections. Those systems become more and more sophisticated all the time. If there are dealerships out there that are not using a DMS software system, phew! How the heck are they compliant? How do they keep up? There are some dealers out there who still try to run things by hand and are fairly successful, but they will never be large.

It's not a good practice to underwrite higher dollar wholesale value cars with low down payments the same way they would with regular Joe Citizen on a lower dollar wholesale car with mid-range down payments.

The main benefit to using a DMS system is that the business can grow much bigger in a controlled environment.

The dealer can control all the moving parts of the business, and manage and see and report what's really happening. It can also be used to demonstrate your ability to control things to future partners and lenders. It's easier to grow the business exponentially, attract business partners, and report to lenders.

In today's economy, especially in the buy-here pay-here space, a good DMS system with a good accounting system is essential. It is a way to demonstrate to lenders who you are and how you operate your business.

Without that support, it's hard to get big money into your business. It's even becoming more difficult on the underwriting side. That is why AutoZoom is such a value to dealers; it is a system that brings them into a world where they don't have to worry about the compliance end of underwriting.

In fact, I would be bold enough to say that buy-here pay-here dealers who aren't on an underwriting system — a scoring system —are violating federal regulation to some degree or another. I say that only because of the perspective that I have been working with one of the largest law firms in the United States and having them check AutoZoom for compliance and learning all the things I've been taught from being in buy-here pay-here for 45 years. I know without a doubt that a lot of dealers out there are not compliant.

## Why systems-driven businesses are more valuable

If an investor is mostly focused on being an investor with money, they don't want to have to get into the business of learning how to be the car guy, or be a buy-here pay-here guru. They don't have time.

Compare it to an investor who wants to buy a McDonald's, but doesn't want to learn how to flip burgers.

Without knowing their winning underwriting formula, it's very difficult for a dealership to maximize sales by expanding that wholesale operating range safely without compromising collectability.

When I want to explain that concept with Texas car dealers who know what Texas Aggies are, I have the following funny conversation: "Do you know what an Aggie explosive mine detector is?" They usually say, "No." "It's a guy (Aggie) standing up, putting his hands over his ears and putting his foot out in front of him trying to find out where the explosive is."

When you're trying to expand your wholesale footprint without a scoring system, it's kind of the same way. You can get hurt out there.

# CHAPTER NINE:

# Benefits of Using Leverage in the Business

I actually still enjoy business — and I enjoy various businesses, but I particularly like the financing end of the buy-here pay-here business.

I never really liked cars because of the way I started as a lot rat. The thing I like about the finance end of the business is that I have the ability to leverage that business. Historically, buy-here pay-here produces a 20 percent revenue — pre-tax profit — and 50 percent return on equity; who wouldn't like that? Who wouldn't appreciate that?

Now most people, especially in high-level banking and professions, wouldn't think that leverage in our industry would be possible because they see buy-here pay-here as extremely high-risk. It's like having brain surgery. There's risk in brain surgery, but having it done by a brand new surgeon who has never done one is riskier than undergoing it with someone who has done a thousand.

It's the same principle with the buy-here pay-here industry — there is risk in the business. However, there's risk in any business. But if the buy-here pay-here business is controlled properly and expenses are managed, it is possible to predictably produce 20 percent of revenue pre-tax profit, and a 50 percent return on equity — if you have leverage. And I mean borrowing money to fund the business rather than using entirely all the capital. I don't know of any other place to invest and get that kind of return on a consistent basis that is dependable and gives the business owner control.

Borrowing money gives leverage in this business, but it needs to be done sensibly. Doing it sensibly means that they're trying to push the limits of the industry, and trying to sell everything they possibly can to the right people.

We recommend that dealers not borrow more than 55 percent or 55 cents on the dollar of principal balance of their total receivables. That sets them up well in case they need to move to another lender. There are many lenders out there who will loan that way.

Or if they are not able to move that loan, they're not so overloaded in debt that they're not able to pay that debt down immediately out of the cash flow if they're in a situation where they have to.

That lesson stuck with us after my parents died and the family inherited the business and we were left with a mess that nearly cost everything because our parents didn't do proper estate planning. Our line of credit was called by the bank.

We built it all back up, and now the family business has an extremely large credit line which has enabled them to become one of the largest, private buy-here pay-here dealerships in the nation.

So many dealers don't know that they should have leverage — or they're afraid of leverage.

# CHAPTER TEN:

# What Big Money?

Many of my successful buy-here pay-here dealer clients on paper make profits. That being said, some of them have asked me the question, "So, I am making all of this money. Where is it?"

My response is, "As long as you are growing your sales volume and adjusting your business model upward, you will be cash poor."

One of the biggest factors contributing to dealers being cash-strapped is the tax law change that took place in the late 1980s. The Retail Installment Sales Act requires that dealers selling and financing vehicles must pay federal income tax on the entire profit of the sale in the same tax year of each sale.

This means that dealers will pay taxes on phantom income unless they circumvent the law via establishing a related finance company that purchases each of the retail installment contracts.

Assume that a dealer takes on the task of forming a related finance company. Just because he has shifted the tax burden to the future does not mean that he has met every challenge related to the funding of his business.

Actual Cash Value (ACV) Creep and Competitive Down Payment pricing will consume much of the high net profits in his buy-here pay-here business if the dealer does not have a good handle on his business model.

Most dealers realize that the wholesale cost of goods for used cars is climbing. But many have yet to realize the negative impact this can have on cash flow when coupled with the natural tendency most dealers have to move up in car cost as they grow their business.

NIADA's Used Car Industry Report 2015 shows that the average ACV, average re-conditioning cost, average down payment and average number of annual retail units sold for 2015 were $6,237, $1,207, $1,089 and $550 respectively. Let's assume that this was a specific dealer's business model. If this dealer had allowed his average ACV including reconditioning cost to move up to $8,500 for 2016, he would have needed an additional $580,800 to fund his 2016 sales. This assumes that the dealer maintained the same average down payment and sales volume as he did in 2016.

However, in most cases when a dealer increases his average ACV, he usually insists on larger down payments. Assuming he did so, he could still have a cash flow challenge. Even if the dealer had produced an average down payment of $1,500 in 2016, his average cash-in-deal would have increased.

In other words, the average ACV including reconditioning cost of $8,500 minus the average down payment of

$1,089 would have required the dealer to risk $7,411 of his capital on each sale. His total 2016 sales would have consumed $4,076,050 in capital.

Using the same math, a dealer's risk for each sale for 2016 would have required $7,411 in capital. Therefore, one can see that the total capital requirement for 2016 sales would have been over $4 million.

Failure to properly control a buy-here pay-here business model can create a cash flow disaster. However, once sales growth levels off for a couple of years and the business model is well established, the dealership can become a cash cow.

# CHAPTER ELEVEN:

## BHPH – License to Print Money

Having spent the last 45-plus years in the buy-here pay-here industry, I have learned that it is a license to print money if properly managed.

My family and I started our first buy-here pay-here lot in 1969 with $500 borrowed money and minimal industry knowledge. Since then, our companies combined efforts have yielded well in excess of $2 billion dollars in total receivables created to date.

Buy-here pay-here is coming of age. Those who learn to manage the risks of the business through the use of tried and true methods and evolving technologies will create fortunes.

When growing a buy-here pay-here business, it is vital to start with or change to the best dealership management software available today. Information is the key to properly managing a buy-here pay-here business.

Additionally, standardized underwriting and buy-here pay-here credit scoring is proving to be a beneficial component for competing in the current market. Customers are becoming more spoiled every day. Prospective buyers are expecting a lot more car for a much lower down payment. Considering the cost of a good used vehicle these days, your company's ability to more consistently and accurately decision deals will determine your degree of success in the future.

In order to maximize your business, consider the following:

## Product range

Many dealers today get a start in buy-here pay-here by offering vehicles with ACVs of $4,500 and less. While the yields associated with those vehicles can be impressive, the challenges related to the vehicle's condition can be cumbersome.

The sweet spot in the industry is an ACV range of $3,500 to $7,500. Realize that the greater the spread between the cost of the low-end and the high-end vehicle, the greater volume and range of customers will be attracted and close. The goal in buy-here pay-here should be to match product range with your ability to fund the business.

## Risk dollars

Markets vary across the nation. Where there is less competition, customers are willing to pay larger down payments. Therefore, dealers are able to recover more of the cost of the vehicle at the time of sale. Contrary to popular belief, the size of down payment has very little to do with the performance of the note, unless you are dealing with extreme low-end customers. Utilizing buy-here pay-here scoring enables dealers to more accurately match customers with dollars at risk or cash-in-deal. Industry leaders are learning to sell more cars for a lot less down.

## Repo rate

In buy-here pay-here, just as in banking, there will be repossessions. Dealers do not create repos. Most repos are a result of the following: good people with poor means and good intentions ultimately not being able to pay in a timely manner, mechanical failure, and/or physical damage. While the repo rate (number of vehicles that ultimately come back as compared to the number sold) is an important factor to measure in your business, a 30 to 45 percent rate is not alarming.

## Repo frequency

Frequency is much more important than repo rate. The months in which the repos occur can make or break a buy-here pay-here dealer. Eighty percent of all repos traditionally occur within the first 18 months of the life of contract originations.

Repos usually peak between the third and sixth month of the installment contracts. Buy-here pay-here scoring enables dealers to build portfolios that have repos peaking in later periods.

To maximize sales, dealers should target a 30 to 45 percent repo rate, coupled with a repo frequency peaking in the sixth to ninth month following retail installment contract originations. A protracted frequency will minimize losses traditionally associated with a higher repo rate.

## Collectability

According to NIADA's Used Car Industry Report 2015, the average net dollar loss rate (% of principle) for 2014 was 26.37%

Through the use of today's technologies, dealers are pushing all the limits in the industry without compromising collectability. Dealers should target collectability in the 80 to 85 percent range or in other words a net dollar loss rate of 15% to 20%, while at the same time pushing the limits on repo rate and properly managing repo frequency in order to maximize sales.

The master plan of buy-here pay-here should be to keep customers paying the dealership for a minimum of 10 to 15 years by providing the broadest range of products for the lowest down payment. Draw on the experience of industry experts and utilize evolving technologies to grow your business. Those who do so may far exceed their wildest expectations of growth in their dealerships, as my family and I did.

# CHAPTER TWELVE:

# BHPH; Feeding the Monster

Long before I ever learned about internal rate of return, effective yield, relational databases, static pool analysis, regression analysis, the differences in repo rate and repo frequency, credit score modeling, audited financial statements, agreed-upon procedures audits, and a plethora of other things associated with building a publicly traded sub-prime automobile financing entity, I worked in my family's buy-here pay-here business from 1969 to 1988. I have experienced difficulties feeding the buy-here pay-here monster from its inception.

We have all heard the saying, "It takes money to make money." Anyone who has created a buy-here pay-here business will say that funding growth in their business is like feeding large amounts of cash to a money-eating monster.

Funding buy-here pay-here operations is becoming more costly every year as vehicle wholesale values continue to increase.

A while ago, I consulted with a dealer who funded his business using very little capital and more than $400,000 in credit card debt. Though everything turned out well for the dealer, I would not say that he used the ideal funding method.

Fortunately, funding sources for dealerships are maturing and meeting the capital needs of larger dealers on a regular basis. Ten million dollar credit lines are no longer unusual in the industry.

## What good is a funding source?

So what good is a funding source geared toward large dealerships if a dealer is just starting out with a few thousand dollars and good credit?

It is not much help now, but it improves one's chances of building a giant company in the future. Individuals who understand the money-making power of buy-here pay-here and are willing to throw everything they have at it stand a chance of becoming a powerhouse someday. Dealers owning automobile accounts receivables with the total principle balance exceeding $5 million are now good candidates for multi-million dollar credit lines.

If a dealer learns the fundamentals of mastering 100 contracts, he possesses the core knowledge to eventually master 1,000 or even 10,000-plus contracts. However, knowing the basic fundamentals of buying, selling and financing vehicles is not enough to secure lines of credit.

Regardless of a dealership's size, the owner must be able to demonstrate to potential capital sources that they understand all aspects of their business. They must be able provide reporting, statistics and analysis in comprehensive formats to secure even small lines of credit, unless the funding source is relying upon assets other than vehicles and auto receivables to secure the dealer's debt.

I have spent much of my time consulting dealers. Many have told me that they started on a whim and/or shoestring. Those who have become most successful were able to demonstrate early on that they had control of all aspects of their business. Many went to friends and family when they first needed more money to feed the buy-here pay-here monster.

Eventually, they moved up to local banks that normally loaned each business less than $1 million. Some built their -customer-base principle balance to above $2 million and were able to demonstrate that they were in control of all aspects of their business. This enabled some to secure multi-million dollar lines of credit.

I have learned that in most cases, dealers who are willing to invest time and money have audited financial statements completed early by regional accounting firms. They will come out far ahead of the others when pursuing large credit lines. Dealers who utilize strong relational database technologies and credit scoring systems have a better understanding of their business and are more able to direct extreme growth that usually goes hand-in-hand with large credit lines.

If you are not taking the action steps required to benefit from a multi-million dollar line of credit now or in the future, I would be glad to talk to you about why you should.

# CHAPTER THIRTEEN:

## AutoZoom and Zoomers

After I had taken that five-year respite from my indirect lending company and its ensuing disaster, I decided to consult with local dealers in my area.

I just sat and talked with them at no charge for an hour or two, just having long conversations. Throughout each conversation, we would identify possibilities of what I could help them with in some areas they struggled in. I told them what my fee would be if we were to do that.

As I started doing that consulting work, I spoke with more dealers, doing the same thing. Ultimately I determined that the biggest challenge that almost everyone faced was in standardizing their underwriting.

Because of my background with my own indirect lending company and everything learned in it, I knew how to build scoring models. I started out building those as part of my consulting and eventually I was doing a lot of that.

At that time, my son Gregory was in the Marines. He and two other guys were in charge of tracking the troops around the world for the Marines because he was an electrical engineer. He's a very bright young man. One day he was sitting with me and said, "Dad, show me what you're doing now."

I told him I was consulting and whatnot, and showed him how I built scoring models for dealers in a localized environment. Dumbfounded, he looked at me and said. "Dad, you know you can do that over the Web."

Here is another time that I was glad that I was open. I said, "Oh my gosh, are you sure?" He assured me that I could. So I started looking for partners who knew technology and could take up that end. After a while I decided that it made sense for me to become partners again with Allen Dobbins of AutoStar and that we would create AutoZoom.

I wish I could say that I was the first who came up with the terminology and idea of scoring models for the buy-here pay-here industry. There was a product called Wonderlic —a family named Wonderlic was building all kinds of scoring models for different industries. They took an entirely different approach than I do about that. But they didn't understand the car sales industry like we do, they didn't have our background. So their business model failed. They got out of the business of building scoring models for used-car financing dealerships.

At the time that I started AutoCredit and then Auto-Zoom, it wasn't because I thought of something that would make me some money and then try to sell it. I identified that there was a need and created a solution.

Here is another interesting story: as I struggled in my father's company and was trying to determine what direction

I wanted to go in life, I paid attention to a lot of things. One was other successful business people, especially billionaires. One day I watched a documentary about H. Ross Perot. At the end, the question was asked, "Ross, what can you tell the folks watching that they should do if they want to become wealthy?"

He looked straight at the camera and said, "If you want to get wealthy, don't reinvent the wheel. Focus on your own industry and find the holes. Fill those and you'll get wealthy."

So I sat there in front of the TV and I thought, *Wait a minute. What are the holes in the buy-here pay-here industry?* The number one hole I identified was that there are never enough cars.

In a geographically limited area, someone can become a pig in the market — let's say they have a high demand for used cars. That person could get known as a greedy person or a company that hogs cars. Used cars are not a commodity. They're not like a can of green beans where the more you buy, the cheaper they get. When someone is perceived as a pig in the market, the market will play against them and car prices will go up. Then they gotta pay more and more to get what they want.

And I thought, *Well how do I solve the problem? If I buy receivables from dealers at point-of-sale at the time they originate the loan, then they can buy their own cars from wherever they need to and nobody's perceived as a pig in the market. That solves that problem.*

The next problem I immediately identified sitting there was that there's never enough money. No matter what anybody's power is for borrowing, it's not easy to borrow it as fast as the business grows. I looked at how to solve that problem.

I started doing a lot of research and determined that asset securitizations were the answer. Eventually, I got around to finding the right kind of partners and that was one of the keys. Using fax machines centralized it and then DMS software was being developed to run companies.

All the pieces and parts came together — and I was paying attention; I was open. That enabled me to create Auto-Credit. That same thing applied to creating AutoZoom. I simply identified a need. The need was identified through consulting; and I thought, *Well if applying that logic brought me to success in my other company, then it should do the same here.* And it did.

Over time, AutoZoom evolved with adjustments because of questions that were asked and the way scoring was done in the beginning. I also applied a lot of what I learned in my indirect lending company. In fact, when I had the indirect lending company, I didn't know a lot about the scoring and building models and doing the things that we know to do today. I had to hire experts to come in that taught us how to interpret our data, even credit agencies.

At one time we had about 20,000 active accounts or more in my indirect lending company. We originated 50,000 loans over a seven-year period. We had a lot of data and a lot to learn. I applied the same kind of rules to developing scoring models, and I originally started out identifying 50 different possible drivers — or categories — that could be possible predictive elements. Through testing a lot of data that came out of that company and narrowing things down through various regression analysis methods and static pool analysis, we determined that we could get a predictive result with using 12 categories as long as we had five ranges of data associated with each of those.

Even now, AutoZoom continues to evolve. It's a never-ending process. The more data we gather, the more we know. We have relationships with more than 800 dealer clients around the nation. Those dealer clients have scored over two million customers through our systems, and they've originated loans on over $14 billion dollars. Not only that, but several hundred thousand repossessions have been identified in our software as a part of what the dealers do, so we're able to see repo economics as they relate to people's scores that tie back to the underwriting criteria.

We get better at it all the time. A dealer who is trying to figure out a scoring model for themselves — which they could do, but it's very difficult —would only know what is going on in their own backyard.

## Picking a name wisely

AutoZoom didn't start out with that name. There is a story behind that. Phew. Tell you what, you live and you learn.

Originally, I did not think I would be in the scoring business long-term. In fact, I thought I would score and consult, but eventually it led to just scoring. My plan was to eventually get back into the indirect lending business and platforming off of my client base.

Money evaporated. Understandably, nobody wanted to do anything after 9/11. That threw me into consulting. So when I created AutoZoom, the name was originally Auto Loan Technologies, LLC. That is still the name of the parent company. The reason I chose that name is because I thought we would call it Auto Loan Tech as our dotcom — AutoLoanTech.com with the idea of eventually getting back into indirect lending.

As time progressed and our focus narrowed in on scoring, we reached a point where our clients couldn't even remember our name. They would say, "Now what's the name of the company? Is it Loan Tech? Tech Loan? Loan Loan? What's the name of the company?"

That was absolute insanity. If our own clients didn't know the name of our company, then our prospects possibly couldn't remember it either.

So again, in my infinite wisdom, I thought I might be better off hiring experts who could help me rebrand my marketing company. I hired a talent I was aware of and we had a branding session. I don't remember the entire process of how we ended up with it, but we landed on AutoZoom.

It fits. We are almost an automatic, we zoom in on the details. It's the essence of who we are. When someone hears the name AutoZoom, they don't forget it.

It was a tremendous boost in our visibility, and in our client's ability to remember us, repeat, and talk about us. Had we not hired that talent, we'd still be stuck and our clients wouldn't know who we are. We wouldn't be where we are today as a company, either.

It's funny, our name has become a verb with some of our clients. Many times I hear them ask their employees, "Did you Zoom that deal?" I've heard that a lot. So within our company we have started referring fondly to our clients as Zoomers, because our Zoomers are zooming deals.

# CHAPTER FOURTEEN:

# What does AutoZoom do?

The main difference between what AutoZoom does and that which used-car financing dealerships are capable, is that we build custom-fit scoring models for each dealer based upon our experiences and the large data sets and testing.

When they use our system, they are using their custom-fit scoring model.

Not only do they have the numeric value that measures the credit quality of the customer in order to guide their decisioning, it also gives the dealers a way to establish benchmarks. For a basic underwriter or a novice underwriter, the upper management can instruct them that if the quality of credit crosses a certain threshold in numeric value, management does not have to get involved.

Not only does the system have a threshold, it saves that numeric value. So in the future when the deal gets flagged as a repossession, the business can enter in information or data as far as date of repossession and its economics.

In that case, because the dealer has captured the repossession in numeric value, they're going to be able to tie the repossession economics to the value that's tied back to the underwriting criteria.

As a result, for the first time ever, that financing dealership then knows their winning underwriting formula.

When we measure the characteristics of someone that a buy-here pay-here dealer is expecting to extend credit to, we've learned either by gut and feel or repetition what the characteristics or personalities of people are who tend to pay better for cars. We call them categories — they are also called drivers.

When I first worked on developing AutoZoom I created a list of nearly 50 potential drivers who were predictors. I did regression analysis and all kinds of study on the 50,000 deals that had originated in my indirect lending company.

Through that, I determined that there are realistically about 12 main drivers or categories that are predictive enough. Some others added a little bit of value, but I needed to narrow it down to about a dozen because 50 would've been way too many.

So in every score sheet that we develop, there are 12 categories or drivers that we have tested through all kinds of fancy analysis and testing against large sets of data to determine the predictive nature of those.

In addition to that, there are five ranges of information associated with each category. For example, a dealer might have five different ranges of income for an individual starting say at $1,200 per month income scaled up to $3,500. Income is different in different parts of the country.

The winning formula in underwriting is what AutoZoom is really geared to do, which is not only produce a numeric value that measures the customer's credit quality, but looks at a secondary measurement that involves five categories and five ranges associated with each of those.

The purpose of our scoring technology is to enable financing dealerships to better match up the credit quality or lack of quality with the right deal structure so that they're not taking more risks than they should. The goal of our AutoZoom system is for dealerships to be able to sell more cars and reduce repossession losses at the same time.

By knowing how to better structure a deal with a weaker customer, they can push them into a lower car-cost vehicle on a wholesale basis and get a larger down payment relative to the wholesale investment.

They can also better analyze and identify the higher-quality credit customer who has higher expectations about getting a greater quality, better equipped, lower mileage car with better terms, better financing, and lower interest rates. There may be a longer term to get a lower down payment requirement.

Not only do we teach the dealer through the scoring system how to sell cars to the general population, but also show them how to buy the credit a little bit deeper in unworthiness as long as they're structured correctly. Really, the primary focus is how to capture that higher quality credit customer and meet their expectations using numerics to make sure everybody's doing that correctly, and that everybody's on the same page.

In the past, some customers may have been financed just by dealers looking at their credit and job history. But there may be other compensating factors. For example, maybe they haven't had the job as long as someone would like or their credit score is really, really bad, but they have a huge down payment. We prefer to measure the potential customer's stability factors. That is different than what the credit bureau measures.

For example, credit agencies measure how many credit cards a person has and how much of the total balance is used up. That's one of the biggest factors in a FICO score. They measure how many times the customer has been late. How far delinquent have they fallen?

We don't measure those things. We do incorporate some of those components off of the credit bureau within our scoring models and bureau score because it is a component. But for the most part we measure almost entirely different things that are more sophisticated because we apply numbers to the process. It's really more along the lines of the way a dealer looks at their deals.

Our system allows the dealer or someone else to make the decision based upon many factors. It allows the dealer to take a day off and trust that someone else can make decisions about financing in the same way they would make it.

Not only that, because they've captured the information and it's Web-delivered, they can access it 24/7 from anywhere. They don't have to dig through the customer's file or be physically present. It is very easy to analyze each transaction as far as credit-worthiness, how the deal was structured, and to hold their employees accountable to doing business in a very controlled way.

Because there is a lot of data over time that helps us determine predictive results, AutoZoom will continue to evolve over time if a new category pops up that's important or we need to adjust it.

As I stated previously, we have relationships with over 800 used-car financing dealers nationwide. To date they have scored in excess of two million customers through AutoZoom by using their custom-fit scoring models. Not only that, they have contracted in excess of one million of those. If you look at the average transaction as far as retail price, it's in excess of $14 billion in loan originations that dealers have put on the books utilizing AutoZoom.

So not only do we have that volume, we also have Zoomer input on several hundred thousand repossessions. All of the economics of those are in the system so that we can aggregate that data and slice it and dice it in a variety of ways so that we get better at understanding the data.

In turn, that directs us to different drivers. In the event that we do come up with different drivers, or categories, we go back and encourage our clients to do a review every 18 months — no longer than 24 months — before adjusting their model or at least looking to see if we need to adjust their models.

# CHAPTER FIFTEEN:

## Most Important Thing for Newbies

The most important tip that I can offer to someone who is new to the buy-here pay-here industry is for them to be open to anything that makes sense as a possible tool to make their business better.

It's easier to run and control a systems-driven business than a personality-driven business. Timely eliminate those systems that don't prove out. After all, there is only so much of a person to spread around with all of the tasks that are part of being in the buy-here pay-here business.

What I mean by a system that doesn't prove out is that there are things for some dealers that don't serve the purpose or get the improvement they expected.

For example, some will use GPS or starter interrupt devices and move away from that technology. Some will try to develop a business development center, what they refer to as a BDC, and either fail to set that up correctly or execute it improperly, and find that it doesn't work for them. So they move on and focus on things that do work.

They might try a DMS software that doesn't meet all of their needs. If they find it doesn't, then they should do more research and find one that does meet more of their needs.

It's the same for the vendors that buy-here pay-here dealers do business with for tire and parts supplies — all of those things. They need to find what works best for them and what the best relationships are.

There are even guys who have tried scoring with AutoZoom and it didn't turn out to be something they envisioned, either due to their lack of understanding or their people not willing to buy into the process, or their unwillingness in general.

We've actually had some upper management and company owners who didn't embrace AutoZoom once they subscribed. They basically say in the beginning that the system makes sense, and then put their people on the technology. But the employees resist it for unknown reasons, so the dealer discontinues subscribing because he did not invest time into learning AutoZoom. Maybe they'll come back another time when they do realize that AutoZoom could've been a solution that they just didn't grasp in the beginning.

Those dealers who are new to the buy-here pay-here business but are coming from traditional retail where they relied upon independent financing will face a massive learning curve, regardless of who they are.

Without a scoring system, they have to go through a lot of money to get that gut sense or whatever they use as to whom to extend credit to or not and how to structure deals.

That learning curve could cost them several million dollars over time, not only in lost money, but in lost potential profits because things weren't structured right.

On the other side of the equation, maybe they tend to be too conservative. They want to make sure they don't take risks, so they have a repo rate that's too low.

The biggest challenge to success happens when numbers haven't been applied to the process.

Let's say you're a new buy-here pay-here dealer. You've done startup and you've done 1,000 deals. You haven't used a scoring system at that point, and you still don't have any idea of what your winning formula is because you haven't applied numbers to evaluate the process and tie it back to repossession analytics.

It doesn't matter if they've done 5,000 deals. They haven't applied numbers to the process and tied them back to repossession analytics, so they still don't know their winning formula.

I have at least one call a month from a dealer who says that they've heard about AutoZoom. Typically the story goes that he's been in the buy-here pay-here business 20, 30, 40 years. His wife loves him, his accountants love him, and his bankers love him because he makes a lot of money.

"But for the life of me," he says, "I don't know what part of the underwriting is making the most money or getting the best results. Can you help me?"

So it isn't just the guys who are brand new and just getting started or haven't started, it's the guys who have been in the business a long time but haven't applied numbers to the process.

# CHAPTER SIXTEEN:

# Messages to Big Dealers

The biggest thing I would say to large buy-here pay-here dealers — even those with multiple locations — is to build up, not out.

What I mean by that is that the overall goal of the business should be to have the highest number of active paying customers on the books relative to fixed overhead. And just stick with that philosophy.

I see a lot of operators out there who think the goal is to have as many stores as they can. But the problem is that they're taking on fixed overhead that can't be reduced easily if they're not getting anticipated results at each location. They're stretching themselves thin because there are new challenges the farther away they get from their geographic central office.

So I always encourage dealers — even the larger ones — to build up, not out. Instead of investing money in a new facility and all the overhead associated with that to the degree that maybe they're holding out for too big of a down payment, I advise to take some of the capital that they're willing to risk in overhead and apply that to reducing the down payment requirements.

For example, they normally wanted to have an average down payment of $1,500 on their cars, but now their target is $1,000 and they sell 100 cars in a month. That costs a lot of money. But the result is that they don't pick up the overhead. The lower down payment requirement to the right customer is the better way to increase their active accounts on the books. That's much better than getting saddled with a bunch of new overhead.

One big thing we help larger dealers with is to continue expanding their wholesale footprint.

For example, my family still owns and operates eight locations of Mike Carlson Motor Company (mcmcauto.com) around Fort Worth that our father started in 1969. When they originally spoke with me about getting on the Auto-Zoom system, they had a mindset of who they were. Their wholesale footprint was roughly $3,000 to $6,000. They'd been in the industry over 30 years at that point.

In a very short period of time by using AutoZoom, they realized that they were not risking high enough dollar cars. The demand was for higher dollar wholesale value cars and they were missing that customer base. Not only that, they weren't willing to sell and finance cars with lower down payments to the higher credit quality customers and thus not meeting that customer's expectations.

So they expanded their wholesale footprint from $3,000 to $6,000 up to $4,000 to $10,000 fairly immediately. That increased tremendously the number of active accounts they were able to keep on the books relative to the number of locations they had.

Over the last 13 years, they've continued to adjust their business model with our help and their wholesale footprint continues to expand. As can now be learned by visiting their company website, they now operate in a wholesale footprint range of $5,000 up to $18,000. You can just imagine the difference that's made.

For an exaggerated comparison, if a dealer is operating in a $2,000 to $3,000 wholesale range car, and that's an example of every piece of inventory they put on the lot, they're going to restrict the number of people who are going to be willing to stop and buy because they don't have much product to offer.

Not only are they going to limit the number of people who come into their store, they're not going to attract the higher credit quality customer. So we always encourage them to continuously expand their wholesale footprint. We also encourage them to borrow money to leverage their business.

I also strongly recommend centralizing underwriting with a fax machine. Well, electronic is in use now and email. I recommend getting all the documentation centralized and *then* collections.

One of the first things that most dealers do is to centralize collections. The improvement there will be noticeable because there is a team to coach and monitor every day. When they're in separate locations, it's a challenge.

Underwriting teams are best separated from sales and from management in each store. They understand their directive and can be coached and monitored more readily every day if they are centralized and especially if they're using AutoZoom.

Dealers really should surround themselves with talent. A lot of dealers have their own talents, but they tend not to have all the people with talent who are necessary to build a sizeable company. They need to be sure to find people who have areas of strength even stronger than themselves in other parts of the operation that aren't their forte.

Another piece of advice for owners of large dealerships is to expand their vision.

For example, I'm asked all the time about our family dealership that is now up to eight locations. They want to know why they haven't expanded to 100-plus like DriveTime.

My answer is that they have all their financial needs met. As a family, they make more money than they ever thought they'd make in their lifetime, and they've been doing well for nearly 50 years. They're passing it on to the third generation now and feel like they've got a very strong business with what they have.

The difference that I also tell dealers is that if they want to go big, they want to go like DriveTime and have over 100 stores — the only difference between them and DriveTime is vision and execution.

That's the main difference between my family's business and DriveTime or even some of the smaller and larger dealers. The market's out there for the taking. If you want to have a multi-million or billion dollar, independent buy-here pay-here operation, you can. It just comes down to answering two questions: "What's your vision?" and, "Are you able to execute?"

# CHAPTER SEVENTEEN:

## Surround Yourself with Talent

It is so important for business owners to surround themselves with talent — especially in-house.

The tendency that I see in a lot of companies is that the owners want to hire people who might have less of an education or less of an understanding of the industry so that they themselves are more comfortable having people around that they deem as beneath them. They don't hire people based on the idea that the more they know, the better they will be.

It's like playing tennis. If you want to get better, you need to play with people who are better than you. If you want to get better at golf, play with people who are better than you. That should be done in every area of business.

For example: in my family's business, they struggled like most dealers with collections for the longest time. They constantly changed out people and got better and better with new leadership.

Ultimately, they were a large enough company so they were able to attract someone to run collections who came out of Chrysler Financial. The person was massively disciplined and made a huge impact in their overall business which was already very profitable. They also had a huge impact in compliance, discipline, earnings, systems, coaching, and teaching.

As far as finding talents outside of the dealer's area of expertise, they should seriously consider hiring talent — whether it's a company or individuals who work on a contract basis to help market the company, help develop strategies for attracting customers, develop websites, develop print material, and develop strategies.

As far as accounting, hire the strongest candidates outside to direct the employees. Find people with talent who have built the best DMS system out there and continue to improve in that area. Don't just get stuck with one because of loyalty when they're not continuing to grow and expand the capacity of that technology, because you'll be stuck.

There are so many things I could tell dealers about the different people available outside of themselves and their company. Always be open. Instead of budget-shopping for talent, look for overall value.

In fact, I make a practice of shopping for overall value. It's no different than buying a car. If you're a guy or gal who appreciates quality, your first choice is not going to buy a Chrysler when you're ready to purchase a vehicle. It depends on your own budget and what you consider the best value, but I think the best value out there in an automobile is Lexus.

Some people don't mind spending the money on a Mercedes or even much higher-end cars than that.

It's all about value and getting what you expect out of it.

# CHAPTER EIGHTEEN:
## Questions Asked and Answered

**"How do I increase my sales without opening more stores?"**

That question almost always comes on the heels of me telling the dealer to build up and not out.

Then we get into who is the dealer who can sell and finance the lowest mileage, best-equipped car for the least down payment, for the longest term, for the smallest payment — to the right customer.

The way to increase sales is meeting the expectations of the better quality customers who are looking for that.

The other way to increase sales is to make the down payment requirement lower.

Well, how do you do that? The answer is to work on getting better financing relationships or bring in more partners with more money. This business will eat money quick. All buy-here pay-here dealers know that pain.

### "How do I grow my business without creating more demand on my time?"

That is a BIG challenge. Anyone who has grown their business to where they either have a high-volume lot, or a large lot with high-volume, or they open multiple locations — each time they open a new store, there is less and less time for family. That is especially true if they haven't centralized underwriting or bought into the idea of having a scoring system like AutoZoom. All the underwriting depends upon the owner or depends upon the team who can only do so much and approve a certain range of gut-feel and basic guidelines.

At the end, the dealer needs to look at all the exception deals while they're running other errands, doing other tasks, going to the courthouse, or going to auctions.

I can't tell you how many dealers I talk to that insist on making the decision on every deal. Even though they have qualified personnel on their lot, they just want that final say. They've got to be on the phone and hear the entire litany of all the qualifying information — whether it's true or not, being properly interpreted or not — over the phone. They still want to make that decision.

So the larger they get, underwriting becomes like an albatross around their neck. That albatross gets fatter and heavier the more volume they do. So they get to where they just don't want to grow their business anymore. Simply because they haven't embraced technologies to take that load off.

They're exchanging their time for more business. It's no different than the common working person. The whole of America has been taught to trade their time for dollars.

That's why, toward the end of their lives, so many people have remorse when they must reduce their lifestyle. They didn't do anything in addition to employment. And they don't like the financial results of retirement because they haven't done all they should have done.

It's the same thing with buy-here pay-here guys. They can only grow the business to a certain size if it's not systems-driven, especially in the underwriting area.

Like I said, it does become like an albatross and a heavy weight around their necks and it reaches a pain tolerance level where it's just too much and they can't grow their business anymore.

**"How do I get good business partners who are willing to fund my business?"**

If you run a buy-here pay-here dealership and are trying to explain to someone who has money that they may possibly want to invest with you, but you aren't able to demonstrate how you make your credit decisions, showing them general basic guidelines is usually not enough. You can't measure the results of general basic guidelines other than by using final results in profitability or collections.

Without a system, the dealer also can't associate or tie back to the repossession economics or what's happening financially in his business to prove that he made the right decisions. He can't demonstrate to his potential partner how he's going to measure and monitor and keep his underwriters under control. That makes potential investors nervous.

## Getting lenders on board

In raising money from investors, there are three things that must be done: show them how they're going to be safe, show them how and when they get their money back, and appeal to their greed. If a dealer hits those three things, they're going to get the money. But the big challenge is how to make them comfortable with the buy-here pay-here business if the dealer can't explain how they make that work and control the underwriting.

### "How do I get lenders to understand my business?"

I can't tell you how many lenders out there for the longest time never could understand this business. It wasn't until in the last 10 years or so that lenders were willing to even come into this space in any kind of big way. They do now because of all the information coming through NIADA's annual industry reports, and through Twenty Groups and industry trade shows. Without that, lenders would never have been able to get on board.

Even still, they're kind of squeamish about loaning money to dealers. It's not because they don't understand the industry so much anymore, but because dealers don't know how to demonstrate how they have control. Lenders like to know that the dealer they loan money to has control so that adjustments can be made as they move forward or when things aren't going the way they should. One of the best ways to control profitability in our industry is to control underwriting.

### "How do I prove to the Consumer Financial Protection Bureau regulators that I'm compliant with the Equal

**Credit Opportunity Act and the Fair Credit Act regulations?"**

The big, sticky wicket for dealers out there right now is proving to the Consumer Financial Protection Bureau (CFPB) regulators that they are compliant with the Equal Credit Opportunity Act and the Fair Credit Act regulations.

Because of the work AutoZoom does in engaging the legal services of Hudson Cook and the time that I spend making sure that we're compliant, I would say that one of the biggest challenges for buy-here pay-here dealers is that they don't have a way to prove that they're compliant. Notice that I said prove.

In fact, I've read many articles reporting that when regulators come in, buy-here pay-here dealers need to be able to demonstrate that they are not violating the nine federally protected classes: race, color, religion, national origin, sex, disability, and familial status. When I speak to dealers about that, a lot of them don't even know what I'm talking about when I say "nine protected classes."

Age can't be used as a way to discriminate against people, whether or not they have been extended credit. Decisions can't be made on whether someone is unmarried and pregnant, upon their national origin or race or ethnic background or religious beliefs or sexual orientation. Plus, there's a whole host of areas that a dealer can get in trouble about there.

Not only that, but the Equal Credit Opportunity Act and the Fair Credit Act have separate sets of regulations that cross over a little bit into each other which creates a lot of confusion. Based on my experience of being in buy-here pay-here and working with car dealers, regulators, and attorneys, I seriously doubt that many dealers out there even come close to complying, because there are habits they have that they don't even realize are against regulations.

The burden of proof of compliance is on the dealer, according to Consumer Financial Protection Bureau regulators.

So many times the dealer is not intentionally doing bad things. But a lot of regulators believe that dealers are out there intentionally trying to be animals. But the fact is, their regulations are so complicated that even a dealer who is trying to do his best to do things the right way has that burden of proof on him.

Unless there is a system like AutoZoom in place, he can't prove up what his systems are, what his decisioning is based upon and how he's not deviating from that, and how he's not hiding things. Without any of that in place, regulators can pretty much just decide what they want to do.

I have been asked if I heard about Bureau officials who found dealers who weren't making standardized decisions and were fined because their decisions led to possible discriminatory results.

Let's put it this way: everyone in the buy-here pay-here business or financing auto receivables should realize that different ethnic groups and cultures are raised, trained, and have grown up in families in different ways. That's just the way it is. Some are more focused on education. Some are lax and don't train their children about how to be smart about finance such as interest rates, paying their bills on time, how to be smart about credit.

Some races and cultures are weaker than others when it comes to knowing how to do business in an intelligent way and keep themselves out of financial trouble.

Bureau regulators even look at the results of some of the financings that go on for people who go to traditional retail lots and get credit through indirect lenders. .

The truth is that people in some cultures don't know that they can debate over a price or fight for a lower interest rate. They don't know about credit-worthiness. So they just accept the sticker price and whatever interest rate is offered. They may accept terms that might be more egregious than what the more educated have settled on. Different cultures and facets of society are trained differently to fight harder for the deals that make more sense.

As a result, CFPB regulators look at the books and say, "Oh, we can tell by this particular race or this particular culture, or this particular societal group that they're not getting as favorable terms as these other groups."

The thing is that it's probably true, but it is not because buy-here pay-here dealers and indirect lenders are being ruthless animals and taking advantage of certain races. It's just the way those races or cultures operate. That's how crazy it is.

But dealers can still be fined. Or regulators are out there trying to fine them when they discover that there's a difference in sales and terms.

The best way for dealers to defend themselves is to have a way to measure and prove to CFPB regulators that they have benchmarks in place with a technological system and that they do not just standardize underwriting. The system proves that not only do they have guidelines set in numeric values that tie back to underwriting criteria; it can be proven through repossession analytics that what they do is predictive in nature to make their credit decisions.

With a system in place, regulators will have cause to believe that the dealer is putting forth their best effort to comply with laws whether or not it is done perfectly. It shows them that the dealer is at least at a higher level of proving that they're trying to comply.

A dealership is in trouble who has nebulous underwriting criteria guidelines that they may or may not stick to and doesn't have a way to prove that their process is predictive.

# CHAPTER NINETEEN:

# AutoZoom Success Stories

When I think about success stories, I have to start with my family's business, Mike Carlson Motor Company (mcmcauto.com) in Fort Worth.

When I first approached them about using AutoZoom, there were a few questions: how can one number, one numeric value, be smarter about making a decision about who to finance — and how to do that? What we know and have learned over the last 30 years in financing over 150,000 deals works just fine. How are the gadgets in this new system possible?

Because we are family, and because they wanted to try to embrace new technology, they walked slowly in the beginning. At first, they didn't even rely on a performance of the system to help them make the decision.

They tracked the activity, they scored every deal that made it to the desk, and they showed every deal that went into contracted status just as a way of measuring how that compared to the decisions they made.

The thing that stood out to them was that they weren't willing to risk enough money on the street after down payment. They weren't willing to take a lot less down payment on higher-quality credit customers. They weren't willing to operate in a high enough wholesale range of vehicle.

But by using the technology of AutoZoom, they very quickly saw that those were areas for improvement. In making those adjustments in the wholesale range instead of operating in the $3,000 to $6,000, moving to more of a $4,000 to $10,000, the number of active accounts at each location dramatically increased over about an 18-month period, or a two-year period. It virtually doubled the active accounts at each location over time.

Bruce Wiltsey is another client. He is President of First Sun Financial. AutoZoom builds indirect lending models too — his company started out as an indirect lender.

At the time he first subscribed to AutoZoom, he was he was doing business with local dealers in Florida. Time was passing and he was trying to get accustomed to using and understanding our technology because there's a learning curve that goes with it.

During that time, a lot of dealers were taking such advantage of him that his business almost went under. In fact, it reached a point where he thought he wanted to get off our technology because it was just another budget item. He was trying to cut his budget and operating expenses to stay in business.

Ultimately, we worked things out with him to pay when he could, and he stayed on the technology, and worked harder to make sure that he understood it was through his willingness to continue to put data into the system and score every deal that we are able to help him identify which dealers took the most advantage of him. He got rid of those bad guys and focused more on buying paper from better dealers. He turned his business around.

Later on, he realized that indirect lending is so competitive in Florida that he decided to move away from that somewhat and get into the buy-here pay-here space where he had control not only of the credit approval process, but also the value of the metal on a wholesale basis — to know what the true metal was worth.

He survived in part because he was on our technology and had a good coach on our end helping him understand what was going on.

Pelican Auto Finance in Pennsylvania is another company that now has made a name for itself in the industry by starting out using AutoZoom. It's another indirect lending company, started out as a small regional. They were so excited to be on our technology. It helped them be systems-driven and to expand more rapidly.

As it is with a lot of indirect lenders that we've done business with in the past, if they grow to a fairly good size they eventually learn from all the processes. When they get big enough, they're able to attract substantial external talents.

That enabled them to eventually move away from us and develop their own internal scoring system. That's another success story.

We have another client in Texas with a number of locations. He was operating in the lower end of the used car market as far as wholesale car cost range. As wise as this guy is, with the large credit line that he has, he didn't quite understand his business and was having a hard time getting a handle on it.

It was through numerous meetings we had online with him explaining the industry that he finally gained some comfort in knowing how to control his business and move it forward.

Another entity in Tennessee started out with one location. After using AutoZoom, they started moving into multiple locations. They were originally in the new car franchise. I think they had as many as 15 new car franchises. Through having a controlled environment of growing their buy-here pay-here business, they have shut down or sold off all of the new car franchises, maybe held on to two or three. Now their entire focus is on buy-here pay-here.

# CHAPTER TWENTY:

## Top Five Questions about AutoZoom

**"Can AutoZoom predict which accounts will default?"**

The answer I always give is that as sophisticated as the FICO score is that comes out of credit agencies — even that will not predict which specific accounts will default.

But just like the FICO score, AutoZoom scores can predict how many will default and not only that, but approximately when, and not only that, what the economic impact of those repossessions will be.

Absolutely we can predict on the whole. But I know of no technology out there that can possibly predict by a numeric value which specific account will fail to pay or which account will repossess. It's not possible.

**"If I already have a low repo rate, can AutoZoom be of any benefit to me?"**

I get that one quite a bit. Or they'll say, "I don't know why I even need AutoZoom because I already have a really low repossession rate."

What surprises most dealers is my answer which is a question, "What is your repossession rate?"

## Low repo rate is not necessarily a good thing

Number one; there are many ways to measure repossession rate, so we first need to get that settled. When we determine that we're on the same page about discussing repo rate and that theirs is indeed really low, we tell them that's not necessarily a good thing.

There's a direct correlation with low repossession rates and missing business.

One discussion we end up having with potential clients is that depending on what part of the country they're in, what kind of markup structure they have on their vehicles, what kind of interest rate they charge, what kind of term, what kind of risk tolerances they have, and what kind of capital structure they have, there are ideal, targeted repossession rates.

Another thing we talk about is that repossession rate by itself is not enough information.

For example, a dealer decides that the way to measure repossession rates is to look at 100 vehicles they delivered on credit. Out of those, how many defaulted over time and became repossessions? Imaging a dealership having an 80 percent repossession rate, meaning that out of every 100 they sold and financed, 80 went bad. That sounds like a total disaster. However, if they all defaulted within the last couple months of the contract, it would be like leasing those vehicles and the dealer would make an absolute fortune.

Don't get me wrong; I'm not advocating an 80 percent repossession rate and I don't know anybody that would want to tolerate that. However, a lot of dealers are shocked by the fact that we tell them that their ideal targeted repossession rate may be 45 percent to maximize sales without compromising collectability. The targeted repo rate may be in the order of 35 to 50 percent, in the normal design of buy-here pay-here depending upon the dollar wholesale value of cars they deal in and how long they are financing.

Of course, the longer they finance, there's a longer time for things to go bad. Some dealers might be surprised that if they're operating in a range of a $7,000 wholesale vehicle up to say a $12,000 wholesale vehicle, and they're willing to sell and finance those cars for on average a $1,500 down payment, they may need to extend the terms to as much as 54 months.

They've got to realize that it's a longer time for things to go bad. As long as the repossession rate doesn't exceed 50 percent and the majority of them don't happen until later in the loan's life, that model can be a fortune-making business.

Many dealers get stuck on repo rate only. What Auto-Zoom can help them do is figure out how to maximize their sales which might increase the repo rate; but the bottom line is that they limit their losses and maximize their profits. It would be nice to have a zero repo rate. However, that just doesn't happen in this industry. The repo rate is only a part of that formula. If you are squeamish about repo rate, maybe you should consider banking.

It's also about the economics of the repossessions and how well the dealer was collateralized and appropriate to the creditworthiness or unworthiness of the customer. How well do they recover on a cash-on-cash basis on the deals that go bad?

I'll give an example of something we use all the time: AmeriCredit, which most everybody's heard of and was eventually sold off to GM Financial, were more of a traditional indirect lending model. If anyone studied their annual reports, they would find that typically their repossession rate out of every 100 they put on the books and financed, is typically 15 to 20 percent. So that means 15 to 20 vehicles out of every 100 fail and become repossessions.

I don't know the timing of all that because I don't have all their information, but I do know that their bad debt would be anywhere from a 6 to 8 percent write-off of bad debt in dollars. That's traditional indirect lending, or sub-prime indirect lending.

Well, in buy-here pay-here, a very good business model is somewhere between a 35 and 45 percent repossession rate with a collectability or bad debt percentage running somewhere on the order of 15 to 20 percent on dollars. There are dealers out there who don't understand that. There are dealers who have a much bigger dollar write-off percentage than that because they don't have control of their underwriting.

There are others out there who think that they're in buy-here pay-here, but actually are not. We can tell by looking at their bad debt percentage, or their repo rate, whether or not they're maximizing the buy-here pay-here space, and/ or maximizing the sales on each geographic location.

**"How can AutoZoom do a better job than me?"**

Dealers tell me they've been in the business 30 or 40 years, they've got this gut feel, and they just want to do the interview process with the customer.

The answer that we always give is that they may already be very good at what they do. The difference between what they're doing is that they are personality-driven rather than systems-driven. The dealer must physically be there, and there isn't a way to demonstrate their winning formula to me or a lender or a partner.

I always put them through the test. I ask how many deals they have originated since inception. Not how many have they decisioned, but how many they have contracted. Usually they tell me anywhere from 500 to 10,000. I tell them that sounds great, they've got a lot of experience at it, and I hear what they're saying, "I've got this."

The dealer tells me that they've got an underwriting gut feel. So I ask them to tell me what their winning formula is. Which of those deals that were originated in the last five years have produced the best economic results relative to the vehicle, the down payment, and the credit quality of the customer?

Their answer is usually, "Uh...I can't." Then my next question is, "How much longer do you want to be in that position? You've got millions of dollars in receivables you're generating, and you don't know your winning formula."

**"I have skilled underwriters who have been with me for many years. Why do I need AutoZoom?"**

That is typically one of the resisting questions in the beginning. Then ultimately, the person who was their champion underwriter that was trained the way they wanted was either pulled out of there by going into partnership with someone else or recruited out of their organization by someone willing to pay them more.

In fact, one underwriter was injured seriously in a car wreck that nearly killed him. He ended up having multiple surgeries on his spine. This was somebody who had been in place at that dealership for more than 15 years.

There was no way that dealer could imagine that the person they depended upon was going to be gone. Fortunately, they were on AutoZoom and slid the second person in command into that person's seat. And because they were on AutoZoom, it was not even noticeable in the business sense that the other person was gone.

Usually the dealers who start out asking that question end up becoming clients.

AutoZoom also catches pattern changes such as the volume of deals being scored.

We'll contact upper management or owners and ask if they realize something we found is going on in their business.

We can see something that's going wrong and get with them. Sometimes it is a situation where it was something they didn't think needed to be monitored because somebody in upper management was doing that. But we called it to their attention and they're so grateful that we followed up. We can see what's going on and what's changing even when they're not looking. So we put them on point and they get things back on track.

**"How can I get past my fear of allowing a system to make underwriting decisions for me?"**

In the first place, AutoZoom never makes the decision. It's simply a custom-fit scoring model specifically built for that dealership. It's a way of measuring the credit quality of the customer, the quality of the deal structure and the overall picture by using those scores as benchmarks. AutoZoom captures those scores to use later to tie to repossession economics.

In the beginning, we have many dealers who absolutely, no matter what documentation we present to them or show them other dealers' data, just can't turn loose of their fear.

So we encourage them to keep doing what they're doing. Keep making credit decisions the way they've been making them, but add the step of scoring every deal that makes it to the desk. Then push those deals into contracted status, so that you can see, as measured by AutoZoom, which customers are being put on the books, what their credit quality is, and how the deals are being structured in the way that they currently operate. Do it for a month. Do it for two months. Do it for 90 days. We've had some dealers do it for as long as a year.

That's extreme, but for the most part, most people trust the system within the first 90 days, especially if we're reviewing the data with them and explaining to them what we say. Because we understand AutoZoom, and we understand the buy-here pay-here space, we can tell them more about their business than they even know. We can do that without even being inside their operation.

Although it's not ever a problem to give dealers all the time they need to decide that AutoZoom works and how to implement the technology into what they do, we do believe that getting it onboard is urgent. The biggest urgency is that without AutoZoom, it is next to impossible for dealers to demonstrate to federal and state regulators that their dealership is compliant with all the regulations related to credit.

Another reason is that without AutoZoom, the financing dealership will never know their winning underwriting formula.

Who wants to have millions of dollars in receivables on the books and not know their formula and not be able to demonstrate it to future partners or lenders, or even someone they want to sell the business to later down the road? It's easier to sell a systems-driven business than it is to sell a personality-driven business.

# CHAPTER TWENTY-ONE:

## How to Succeed in Buy-Here Pay-Here

Number one, to become a successful dealer in the buy-here pay-here industry, become a student of the buy-here pay-here industry.

Whether that means reading everything you can get your hands on in publications that come out of trade associations, or attending state and national trade shows like NABD.

The National Independent Auto Dealers Association puts on a national trade show every year. Join a Twenty Group — there are a number of those out there. NCM and NIADA have their own Twenty Groups — those are two that I know of.

Be proactive. Don't sit back and wait and hope for things to change or improve. Be proactive about improving on an ongoing basis. Be diligent.

Most of the guys I deal with today stumble into this business. A lot of them didn't fit into other traditional businesses; they didn't fit as employees and they started selling cars on the side. Next thing they knew, they're doing retail, and they have deals that they can't get financed so they carry loans themselves.

They like the feel of that, so they start doing more of those, and the next thing they know they're getting buy-here pay-here customers. All of a sudden they get family involved, get money from family, get money from partners, and they get some leverage in the business.

Now they're in a business that they never intended to be in, but it's because maybe they were misfits. Maybe they didn't fit into normal, traditional businesses, or they had an entrepreneurial spirit but didn't have a true employee spirit in them.

## The BHPH personality is a lot more creative...

I believe that one reason a lot of buy-here pay-here dealers go into the business is that their personality tends to be a lot more creative and entrepreneurial than a franchise dealer.

They weren't trained in business and they didn't grow up as first, second, or third-generation franchise owners. Most of them have not had traditional college; for certain they haven't gone to business school, they don't need accounting backgrounds, they don't have sophisticated business backgrounds, so they have to learn from the school of hard knocks.

They need to develop 10,000 personalities to deal with all the vendors, customers, and challenges that come such as good customers, bad customers, and all the federal and state regulations. They have to wear many, many hats. We all laugh about that — buy-here pay-here dealers learn to wear many hats.

By far, being a buy-here pay-here dealer can be more challenging than being a franchise dealer.

There are not standard guidelines and baselines that help them like there are for the new car franchise dealers and manufacturers. There are no guidelines. For the longest time there was nothing to help anyone understand how to do anything.

But what I do know is that if you were to take five guys and give them $5 million and parachute them all over the United States, dump them out at different spots, tell them that their instruction is to get in the car business to finance people with substandard credit, "Here's your money, go figure it out," five years later, they will all be doing business similarly. Not the same exact way, but similarly, because customers teach them how the market works and what the demand is.

## Be open, willing and quick

One real big thing is to be open to new ideas. Even the guys who have been in the business for a very long time don't know everything there is to know. I've been doing this since 1969 in a very big way, in many different ways, and I learn new things EVERY day. None of them really surprise me, but sometimes something catches me off guard and it's like, "Wow, I never thought of that!"

Be the one who decides to stop doing things the old way just because that's the way it's always been done.

Holding onto the old way "just because" is one of the biggest mistakes dealers can make.

Be willing to change. Not only be willing to change and improve, but be quick about it. Sometimes changes take way too long and then your competition gets the edge. Be quick to make the change. Do your due diligence and make the decision to either do it or don't do it.

And remember, it's not the big that eat the little. It's the fast that eat the slow.

For example, think about the giant, cumbersome companies in the world that have failed.

They were so burdened with upper management and things that went along with being a huge company that they couldn't move quickly in their decisions. All of a sudden a business in the same industry that's a fraction of their size moved a lot faster.

That will happen in the buy-here pay-here space as well. The smaller business was nimble, and not necessarily due to their size. It may be their philosophy. The fast ate the slow.

One reason I tell that story is because a lot of car dealers think they have a vision for what they can accomplish, and that once they get there they can move the goal up, move it up, move it up — but their first vision was nowhere near what's possible in this industry.

# CHAPTER TWENTY-TWO:

## You Might Be a Zoomer If...

I was speaking at a convention and trying to determine – you know, like when you're in a room and trying to get somebody's attention – what do these people care about? Well, I knew they cared about what can help them. In fact, at some point or another, everybody listens to the same radio station: WIIFM —What's In It For Me?

Losing the audience can happen when you're trying to explain complex figures, analytics, scoring, and things like that; it just kind of goes over the top for most people. When they tune in to WIIFM, you're about to lose them.

So there I was in front of the room, standing in front of a good-size group of people, and I thought: *What's the best way to get and hold their attention?* I decided to have some fun. I remembered being at a comedy club in Fort Worth about 30 years earlier watching Jeff Foxworthy who was just starting out.

He came to a local club called the Funny Bone probably a dozen times. I knew then what the rest of the world would soon know: he is one of the funniest guys on stage. He had a whole series of jokes about rednecks and he always kept his act clean. One of his lines went something like this: *If your family tree doesn't look like a fork, youuuuuuuuu might be a redneck!*

And then I got to thinking, those lines get and hold attention quickly for two reasons. One, they're obviously funny, and two; they create a sense of community and camaraderie. I thought, I *don't need to yell at these guys to pay attention. I just need to talk to them about the pain they may be suffering in the buy-here-pay-here business.*

I have been in this business for over 45 years and I can tell you that I have struggled through some of the same pains and frustrations they have. I knew I could get their attention a-la Jeff Foxworthy and came up with lines like:

- If you want to increase sales, you might want to be a Zoomer
- If you have concerns about your Credit Manager or fear that he or she might leave, you might want to be a Zoomer
- If you feel like you're too far removed from underwriting, you might want to be a Zoomer
- If your repo rate is too low or too high might want to be a Zoomer

Well, I started going through my list of "you might want to be" lines, and something interesting started to happen.

Those folks were there to learn about boring compliance. But the next thing I knew, some of them caught on and mouthed or even said out loud the punch line, "...you might want to be a Zoomer!"

They were really getting into it and it was quite fun. I have to tell you it was the most fun I have ever had introducing AutoZoom to people. You can bet I'm going to continue doing it. It got their attention.

Here are a few more:

- If you're putting more and more money on the street as car costs are going up, and you need to adjust your underwriting but don't know how, you might want to be a Zoomer

- If you're a buy-here pay-here dealer or a startup, or brand new to the business, or you just want to open more lots, you want to be a Zoomer

- If you're the person who has been in business for a long time but still don't know what your winning underwriting formula is, you want to be a Zoomer

So it went on and on and on and we had a lot of fun with it.

I'll share something else about how AutoZoom got started.

I had been out of my indirect-lending venture for around five years when I decided to start doing consulting work with car dealers. It didn't take long to figure out there was a real need for standardization in the underwriting process and the scoring system, especially if you could do it online. I knew such a process would help a lot of guys. And so I went down that path of developing it.

I formed a new company, called it Auto Loan Technologies and started building a client base. We often referred to ourselves as ALT or, like in our web address autoloantech. com, as simply Auto Loan Tech. It's no wonder that people were confused about our name. Even our own clients, some who had been with us two or three years, asked, "Now, what's the name of your company?"

I knew it was a terrible name; we needed an identity. So I hired a marketing firm. They helped me identify and create all the white boards and language. I spent three days telling them about us and what we do. They came up with AutoZoom as a brand and a name. That name captured the essence of what we do with the auto industry: speed and zoom.

And I'm so glad we came up with Zoom. Our customers are more than just numbers. We've created a following, a fan base and a community around our product and service. For example, our clients can go to a dealer convention and when they mingle I have no doubt people will hear things like, "Did you Zoom that?"

## What defines a Zoomer?

Lady Gaga calls her fans Little Monsters. Doesn't sound like a compliment, but they love it. They absolutely love it. So if a dealer can create that same thing with their name and brand, I think that's terrific. It's like being part of a fraternity, part of the "in crowd."

How do we define a Zoomer? A Zoomer is anyone who utilizes our system. It's anyone who contacts us for support or asks us to review their data. A Zoomer relies and depends upon us to be a part of their team, to support them. We interact with each other. That's a Zoomer.

Typically, a Zoomer refers to a dealer or someone who is in the auto dealership business. It is somebody who has at least a hundred active receivables accounts on the books. They are not stodgy or stagnant; they want to grow their business. Even if they're small, they recognize they can benefit from AutoZoom – especially if they are a start-up.

Some who are new to this business have tried to figure out buy-here pay-here and underwriting on their own. Trying to learn the math and match the right risk of money to the right risk of customer while competing head-to-head with other dealers can be an extremely expensive learning curve.

Zoomers can be anyone from a single individual starting up something to a small dealer and up to someone who oversees a dealership chain. Our largest client has a dozen locations. My own family has been in the business since 1969. They started with $500 borrowed money and to date they have financed about 125,000 customers utilizing their own company money. They were early adopters to Auto-Zoom and have been Zooming for 13 years now. They, like many others, wouldn't think about being without the system.

To be a success in buy-here pay-here or anything in life, be willing to work hard, be true to yourself and the people around you and — you might want to be a Zoomer.

~ *Scott Carlson*